Estate Planning: The Fundamental Concepts Under Missouri Law

A General Overview

By Michael E. Magliari

Fourth Edition

ISBN 978-0-9801487-3-2

Printed in the United States of America

First Edition 2011
Second Edition 2014
Third Edition 2016
Fourth Edition 2018

ESTATE PLANNING:
THE FUNDAMENTAL CONCEPTS

TABLE OF CONTENTS

* These chapters have been modified, appended to, and a new chapter added by the supplemental material. Please refer to both sections for a more complete analysis.

INTRODUCTION

For over a quarter of a century, clients, financial advisors, attorneys and accountants have asked whether or not there was a **simple yet comprehensive** pamphlet or book they could read that covered the basics of estate planning. As with any body of knowledge, very basic explanations do not answer many of the questions the inquirer may have; on the other hand, detailed explanations are too confusing and often leave more questions than answers. Without expert commentary, estate planning can be misunderstood and result in miscomprehension and mistakes. This simple book will attempt to comprehensively address the major issues, tools, and techniques currently used to properly manage, transfer, and retain a person's estate for that person's intended purposes.

In order to understand any subject, a student must first grasp the **rudimentary concepts** upon which the entire body of knowledge is based. Likewise, in order to understand estate planning, the reader must first have a firm comprehension of why it is necessary to establish a plan for his or her finances and family.

First of all, a person must realize that chance will not result in financial order; an intelligent **design** must guide the underlying actions and direction of an estate. To have no plan will result in disorganization, financial breakdown, and overtaxation. To neglect the construction of an estate plan is to show a lack of concern toward one's family, friends, and community. The end result is always heartache, stress, and confusion.

Planning first means **organizing** one's assets and gathering vital information concerning a person's financial goals. This requires the individual to organize his or her thoughts and prioritize life goals within his or her unique worldview. Each and every asset a person has acquired, including property interests, must be addressed in a properly constructed estate plan. All of one's estate will be managed and ultimately transferred under the plan, so the plan must be comprehensive in nature.

In a nutshell, **estate planning** can be defined as the preparation for the orderly transfer of one's assets and provision for the payment of one's liabilities, during life and at death, in accordance with the creator's desires. To be granted ownership, control, or dominion over a property interest and then refuse to organize it in a meaningful manner demonstrates a disregard for the privilege so granted.

There are many commonly voiced reasons to prepare an estate plan. Some of the more important **reasons** include the following: (1) the desire to avoid unnecessary court involvement through the probate and conservatorship process; (2) the desire to maintain private records rather than subjecting the estate plan to the public domain; (3) the desire to choose exactly who will manage and eventually settle the estate during life and after death; (4) to determine who will care for children and loved ones; (5) to determine precisely how estate assets, including real estate and personal property, should be held and/or distributed; (6) the desire to take into account certain contingencies that may occur as circumstances change; (7) the desire to reduce taxation within the parameters of current law; (8) the desire to make charitable and personal gifts during life and at death; (9) the desire to provide guidance to one's family in order to foster the family's well-being; and (10) the desire to shelter funds from predators and creditors.

Before reviewing the techniques available to the estate planner, it is necessary to define and understand what an **estate** is. Basically, one's estate is everything a person owns at death, including certain assets owned prior to death. Both state and federal laws define property ownership. The Internal Revenue Code specifically lists the transfers, rights, and powers that define ownership and give rise to inclusion and taxation in one's estate (IRC Sec. 2035-2042). This includes (1) all property that a person transferred as **gifts** within three years of his or her death; (2) the value of any interest that a person has retained for his or her life, including the **possession, enjoyment, or right to income** that is included in one's estate (for example, the right-to-vote shares of transferred stock, even if only a small percentage of the stock, is considered to be the retention of the enjoyment of the transferred property); (3) the value of all property transferred where the interest may return to the person or in which the person may **retain a power to dispose of** the property; (4) the value of any property in which the enjoyment was subject to change through the **power to alter, amend, revoke**, or terminate an interest; (5) the value of an **annuity payment** receivable by any beneficiary based on a person's death (for example, the payment of benefits under an annuity, retirement plan, bonus, or profit-sharing plan); (6) the value of a person's **interest in joint property**; (7) the value of property that a person may appoint to someone else or to which a person may direct the disposition of the property, (for example, if a person may direct property to be used for himself or herself, his or her estate, or his or her creditors, it is deemed to be that person's property); and (8) the value of **all insurance** possessed or owned by the decedent at his or her death.

Generally, a person's estate includes all property that a person has a right to direct and control and each asset in which a person has a beneficial interest. For example, real estate titled in a person's name is included in that person's estate, as well as all financial and investment accounts. All business interests and voting rights are included in one's estate. All interests held in trust that a person has a right to amend, revoke, appoint, enjoy, and dispose of without limitation are included in one's estate. All tangible personal property such as jewelry, artwork, and collections are also included in one's estate.

Like all other fields of knowledge, there are several terms that are customarily used but are not commonly understood. For example, a person who establishes a will is referred to as a **testator or testatrix**, a person who creates a power of attorney is known as a **principal**, and a person who creates a trust is a **settlor**, grantor, or trustor. Likewise, a person who administers a will under a probate process is referred to as a **personal representative**, a person who acts under a power of attorney is referred to as an agent or **attorney-in-fact**, and the administrator of a trust is known as the **trustee**. All of these terms can be confusing, and many of them have similar meanings under various documents.

It is also important to distinguish between general terms such as estate plan, estate documents, and estate asset retitling. The estate plan is the overall theory to be applied to one's estate. This should be thought through carefully and after considering all important contingencies. The estate documents should reflect the estate plan by delineating the **intentions** and dispositions of the creator of the plan. Finally, the estate assets must be positioned and titled in a manner that will carry out the estate plan in accordance with the corresponding documents.

In order for any estate plan to be successful, it is necessary that the person first becomes educated as to the techniques and options available. Next, the person must construct documents that carry out his or her desires and plans. It is important that all estate planning **documents are coordinated** and state precisely what was intended. Lastly, every estate plan must be properly implemented by ensuring that the plan is properly **funded**. Being a proper steward of one's estate requires constant monitoring and reviewing of his or her estate plan.

Although the court system fundamentally tries to carry out the individual person's intentions, the court will necessarily need to rely on the estate documents to interpret the individual's desires. The estate documents will also set the parameters to which the state and federal transfer and **tax laws** apply. In an effort to comply with changing case law, legislative policy changes, and the evolution of legal concepts, the rules governing estate planning are in a state of constant flux. This requires the person to continually **monitor** his or her estate plan. This booklet will refer to the Missouri Uniform Trust Code **(MUTC)**, the Missouri Revised Statutes **(R.S.Mo.)**, and to the Internal Revenue Code of 1986 as amended **(IRC)**. Although some statutes may be cited, the purpose of this work is to give a general and overall explanation of the most common estate planning techniques currently available.

People's lives are also in a constant state of change, requiring estate plans, documents, and asset positioning to be **modified** on an ongoing basis. A review of those persons or entities named as beneficiaries, guardians, agents, trustees, personal representatives, and protectors should be made on a periodic basis.

Those who fail to plan are those who plan to fail. Without a vision, dream, or goal, an individual will be directed by circumstances and become a victim of chance rather than constructing his or her own destiny. On the other hand, those who **take the time to plan increase their probability of succeeding** in life and obtaining the ability to fulfill their goals. As a result of planning, an individual more effectively protects and enriches the lives of his or her loved ones. This is the reason for an estate plan. This is the reason to be diligent in the estate that has been acquired.

CHAPTER ONE – ESTATE FUNDAMENTALS

Whether a person has great wealth or is simply starting out in his or her financial life, some type of estate plan should be thought through and prepared. When a person makes plans for his or her life, reason dictates that the person would decide what is most important and plan accordingly.

GUARDIANSHIP OVER CHILDREN

Q & A

Question 1: What happens if a parent dies without designating a guardian?
Answer: The division of family services and the court will appoint a guardian, and the child may be placed in the foster care system.

Question 2: How does a parent designate a guardian?
Answer: A guardian is designated through a parent's last will and testament.

Question 3: Who can be a guardian?
Answer: Anyone who is designated under a will and who has reached the age of 18 may be a guardian.

Question 4: Who will manage assets that have been left for the benefit of a child?

Answer: The court will appoint a conservator to manage the assets of a minor child who is under the age of 18 unless you make other plans.

For most people, the determination of who would take custody of their children if they could not act is of primary importance. Therefore, the selection of guardians should be the first consideration when an individual has **children**.

Prior to a parent's death, a designation may be made to another person regarding the care of a minor for a limited time. A lifetime designation of custody must be done under a power of attorney by a signed and witnessed designation. Typically, the father and mother have equal rights over the custody of a child, and preference will be given to the **surviving parent** upon the death of either one. Application for guardianship may be limited to school registration or insurance coverage.

The selection of a guardian after a parent's death is made under a person's last will and testament. The placement of children as a matter of public policy is reserved to the courts, which endeavor to not only carry out the wishes of the parents, but also to ensure that the children have the best possible care. This process is directed by the state's guardianship law R.S.Mo. Sections 475.010-340.

In order to become the legal guardian for a child, a petition must be submitted to the court. Letters granting the right to act as the guardian must be given by the court to the individual making the request. The guardian must be **18** years old (an adult) and must be the most suitable person to serve. After a guardian has been appointed, an annual report must be submitted to the court explaining the status of the child.

In the event that the minor has assets available to him or her, the court may appoint a **conservator** who will be given legal authority to manage the child's funds. The probate court will determine how the child's assets can be invested and will require the conservator to give a detailed annual accounting of the income earned and disbursements made on behalf of the child.

The court also retains jurisdiction over adults who are disabled or incapacitated and may appoint a guardian over such a person. For these purposes, a **disabled** person is one who is unable, by reason of a physical or mental condition, to receive or evaluate information or to communicate decisions to such an extent that the person lacks the *ability to manage his or her financial estate.* An **incapacitated** person is one who is unable, by reason of any physical or mental condition, to receive and evaluate information or to communicate decisions to such an extent that he or she lacks *capacity to meet essential requirements for food, clothing, shelter, safety, or other care such that physical injury is likely to occur.* In either instance, the court may adjudicate a person partially disabled or incapacitated.

In the event that a person has not prepared a health care or financial power of attorney, the court will need to appoint a guardian or conservator to manage an individual's assets and to ensure the care of him or her. In the event that a parent has not nominated a guardian in his or her last will and testament, the court will be required to appoint a guardian of its choice with the assistance of the local social services and foster care agencies.

JOINT OWNERSHIP, DEEDS, AND LIFE ESTATES

Q & A

Question 1: Can individuals hold property together and designate who will receive their shares at their respective deaths?
Answer: Yes. Individuals may hold property interests together as tenants in common, each leaving his or her shares to the heirs or designees.

Question 2: Is property held by joint tenants disposed of by the owner's will?
Answer: Not until the last tenant's death. As each joint tenant dies, the respective shares are transferred to the surviving tenant(s).

Question 3: Can a person use property for his or her lifetime and designate someone to receive the use of that property after his or her death?
Answer: Yes; a person can have a life estate in property while another person waits to receive an interest in the property that remains after the first person's death. The designation, however, is generally simple in nature compared to interest held in trust.

As a matter of law, two or more persons may own real or personal property jointly. The manner of the owners' relationship and the designation of title will control how the property is managed and eventually distributed. Property may be held as tenants in common, joint tenants with rights of survivorship, or as joint tenants by the entireties, e.g., husband and wife.

If property is held as **tenants in common**, each owner has a share of the property that may be distributed separately from the other owner's interests without the consent of the other owner(s). In this instance, each share may be transferred during life, through probate at death, or be held in trust. Furthermore, each party's interest may be attached by each party's creditors or predators.

Property held as **joint tenants with rights of survivorship** is held as an undivided interest, with the surviving owner taking title to the entire property interest after the death of the other owners. During the joint tenant's life only transfers with the consent of the other owners are valid. This type of property interest can only be transferred after the death of the surviving tenant through either the probate process, beneficiary designation, or in trust. However, this type of property may be attached by creditors, and, if the judgment is not satisfied, the court may order that the property be sold under a suit for partition.

A unique type of joint ownership between a husband and wife is **entireties** property. This type of ownership vests the interest in the surviving tenant at death and gives complete protection against creditors during the lives of the husband and wife, absent any fraud in the formation of it. This protection evolves from the concept of a husband and wife taking title as one unified person. Under this concept, the property interest cannot be severed unilaterally by one party, and neither can a third party creditor sever the unity based upon only one party's liability.

Many people have a rudimentary awareness of these types of property interests and rely upon joint tenancy to transfer their interest upon one party's death free of probate. However, this will not allow the parties to avoid the probate process if both parties die or upon the survivor's death. For the most part, joint ownership is inflexible and does not allow for the fine-tuning of an estate. In fact, joint ownership, if not properly coordinated with the rest of an estate, will **supersede** other plans and possibly defeat what was truly intended. Furthermore, joint ownership may subject property rights to unanticipated creditor or marital rights of the owners. In many instances, property cannot be transferred without all of the joint tenants' signatures, which may result in a stalemate. If an estate needs to be separated for transfer tax purposes, holding assets in joint name may defeat the tax planning that would have been possible. Accordingly, as an estate planning device, the use of joint ownership is an oversimplified method of transferring assets without considering the contingencies that life may bring.

With regard to the transfer of real estate, many people hold their properties jointly as tenants in common or as joint tenants with rights of survivorship, expecting their interests to automatically be transferred at their deaths. Unfortunately, the circumstances do not always allow the transfer to be accomplished as anticipated.

In order to take into account certain contingencies, the law allows property interests to be held for life with the remaining interest transferred at the death of the life tenant. This is known as a **life estate**. Although the legal theory is sound, the drafting of the terms of a life estate are many times oversimplified and leave the property interest uncertain.

The Non-Probate Transfer Act allows property interests of all types to be transferred through a beneficiary designation. For real property, beneficiary deeds will allow detailed beneficiary designations to be placed on a deed that will only transfer the interest upon the death of the owner. In most instances, this designation is superior to a life estate and a remainder interest. Both of these designations, including life estates and beneficiary deeds, are somewhat limited in scope, may not address necessary contingencies, and may provide only a temporary solution.

NON-PROBATE TRANSFERS

Q & A

Question 1: Can an owner of property designate a beneficiary to that property to take effect at the time of his or her death?

Answer: Yes. An owner of property may list an individual or multiple persons as beneficiaries on all types of properties. This designation is accomplished by a pay on death (POD) or transfer on death (TOD) designation.

Question 2: On what types of properties can POD or TOD designations be made?
Answer: All types of financial accounts, real estate, automobiles, and tangible personal property.

Question 3: Can a TOD or POD designation be challenged?
Answer: Yes. The law allows an interested party to set aside a non-probate transfer. The process can be very complicated, depending upon how the designation was made.

Many states have passed the Non-Probate Transfer Act, i.e., R.S.Mo. Sections 461.001-300, which attempts to circumvent the probate process by allowing **beneficiary designations** to be placed on all types of property interests. This is accomplished by designating that an interest be transferred on death (TOD), such as an automobile, deed, or stock certificate, or paid on death (POD), such as a bank account.

All of the provisions of the non-probate transfer law are exempt from the requirements of the probate code concerning wills. The law requires that a separate writing or instrument be executed that will designate to whom property will pass on the decedent's death. If this is done correctly, the probate process will be avoided. This type of designation can transfer the decedent's interest in many assets, such as insurance contracts, employment contracts, stocks, bonds, mortgages, notes, deposit agreements, compensation plans, retirement accounts, trust agreements, real estate, gifts, assignments, and ownership interests of all types.

The Non-Probate Transfer Act is, however, subject to the rules imposed by the transferring entity, such as a bank or other financial firm. These rules must be contained in a contract and are subject to the **entity's consent and registration**. When a transferring entity accepts a beneficiary designation, the acceptance constitutes an agreement to transfer the title to the property as designated upon the decedent's death. A deed that conveys an interest in real property to a grantee (i.e., beneficiary) upon the death of the owner is effective if the deed is executed and filed with the recorder of deeds prior to the death of the owner.

Tangible personal property may also be transferred under the act by a deed of gift, bill of sale, or other writing. This transfer must expressly state that the transfer will not take effect until after the death of the owner; it must also be specific and be acknowledged before a notary public.

All non-probate transfers are subject to the owner's **right to revoke or change** the beneficiary designation. Therefore, prior to the owner's death, a beneficiary has no right to the property by reason of the beneficiary designation. Upon the death of a joint owner, the surviving owner will retain all incidents of ownership, and the property will not be transferred to the named beneficiary until the death of the surviving owner.

A subsequent beneficiary designation will revoke a prior designation unless provided for otherwise or excepted by the rules of the transferring entity. In order for an agent or attorney-in-fact to change a beneficiary designation, the power of attorney or governing instrument must authorize such an act. The transferring entity may rely on a death certificate and has no duty to verify the information made under oath. The transferring entity does not have the duty to give notice of the manner of the transfer to the person to whom the transfer is to be made, nor is the entity required to locate any beneficiary.

A beneficiary who takes an owner's interest in property at death takes the owner's interest subject to all conveyances, contracts, setoffs, easements, liens, and security interests (i.e., mortgage). Unless otherwise designated, an individual who is a beneficiary of a non-probate transfer must survive the owner's death by 120 hours (5 days). The beneficiary designation may, however, provide for an alternate disposition or contingent beneficiary if the beneficiary does not survive the owner. Such an alternate designation may be the beneficiary's lineal descendants per stirpes **(LDPS)**.

Like all other transfers, a non-probate transfer may be set aside based upon fraud, duress, or undue influence. This must be proven after a petition has been filed with the court by an interested party. Notwithstanding the same, no probate law intended to protect a spouse or child from unintentional disinheritance applies to a non-probate transfer. A deceased owner's creditors, surviving spouse, and unmarried minor children all have rights with respect to the property passing by non-probate transfers, and each recipient of a **recoverable transfer** of a decedent's property is liable for a pro rata share of the property received. Such an action to recover assets must be commenced within **18** months following the decedent's death and be enforced by the decedent's personal representative under a probate administration.

The beneficiary designation may provide for one or more beneficiaries and may designate percentages or fractional shares. Generally, however, the designation must be relatively simple and cannot take too many variables into account, unlike a well-drafted will or trust agreement. A properly crafted estate plan should take advantage of the Non-Probate Transfer Act but shall not rely on it exclusively. Beneficiary designations must be made in conjunction with the overall estate plan but should not replace it.

WILLS AND PROBATE TRANSFERS

Q & A

Question 1: What happens if an owner of property dies without a beneficiary designation or a will?
Answer: The law has designated heirs for every person. Those heirs will receive the property through a probate process known as intestate succession.

Question 2: Who has rights in a decedent's estate?
Answer: Generally, the spouse and children of a decedent have rights to certain shares and support from a person's probate estate.

Question 3: Does every estate need to have a personal representative/executor appointed?
Answer: No. Small estates under $40,000 in value may be probated with relative ease.

Question 4: Who gets paid to probate an estate?
Answer: The personal representative and the attorney are paid a minimum fee from the estate.

Question 5: If a person dies with a will, do they avoid probate?
Answer: No

Most people assume that when they die, the estate they have accumulated will be transferred through their last will and testament. Those who fail to plan would be surprised to know that the state in which they reside has provided for the transfer pursuant to the **intestate succession** laws of that state, e.g., R.S.Mo. Section 474.010. For example, if there is a surviving spouse, he or she will receive the first $20,000 plus one-half of the estate, and if there are children of the same marriage, those children will receive the other half of the estate.

Under the intestate succession laws, the rules of descent and distribution are set forth so that the decedent's **heirs** are determined. The law determines how the decedent's heirs receive the estate in equal degrees based upon consanguinity (bloodline). The law provides for half-blood heirs and for those children who may have been born after the death of the decedent. The law also addresses advancements of inheritances that may have been designated, as well as gifts in fraud of marital rights.

In the event that the decedent prepared a **will**, his or her estate will be administered pursuant to the terms and conditions of the will with the oversight of the probate court. The probate court will issue letters testamentary authorizing the personal representative to collect the estate assets and to prepare an inventory of them. The probate code allows for elections by unintentionally omitted children and an omitted spouse to take a **share against the will**. All of these elections must adhere to specific procedures.

In order for a person's will be honored by the probate court, it must be correctly prepared, signed, witnessed, and properly notarized. Each state's laws concerning the execution of wills are different, and care must be taken for the terms of the will to be properly implemented. The will, at the very least, should address (1) the beneficiaries, (2) the payment of taxes, (3) the court procedure to be used, (4) the naming and bonding of the personal representative, (5) the naming of guardians, and (6) the sale of property. Many of these designations are more technical than the layperson may suppose and should only be constructed by someone licensed to practice law and who is familiar with the probate practice.

The probate code does provide for instances when the opening of a full estate with a personal representative being named is not necessary. Probate administration may be dispensed with when the estate value is less than the exempt property and allowances granted by the court, e.g., $7,500-$15,000. In this event, a creditor or creditors (such as those who have paid the funeral bills) may request that the estate assets be paid to them in order to be reimbursed for the estate's liability. This type of procedure is commonly referred to as a "**refusal of letters**," meaning the estate is too small to issue letters authorizing a personal representative.

In the event that the estate does not reach the $40,000 threshold of a full probate administration, the law provides for the collection of a **small estate**. This procedure allows an affiant to declare the assets of an estate and request that the court distribute those assets to either the heirs or those persons or entities designated under the decedent's will. This procedure will most likely require both the filing of a surety bond and the affiant's statement that all unpaid debts will be paid. By using the small estate procedure, the lengthy procedure required under a full probate administration can be avoided.

Under a **full probate administration**, the personal representative must submit an **inventory** of the estate to the court within 30 days of being appointed. If the will waived the requirement of a bond, none will be required. The court will publish **notice** in the local newspaper giving creditors the ability to file claims against the estate. This notice will start a **six-month time period** in which creditors can file claims and a spouse could file a forced share election against the estate. During this time, bills, taxes, and expenses should be accounted for and paid. It will also be necessary to liquidate assets or hold them for later transfers.

After the probate estate has run its course, the personal representative will need to file a **settlement** in a supervised administration or a **statement of account** in an independent administration with the court. These will need to be accompanied by **receipts** signed by the beneficiaries showing that they did, in fact, receive their inheritance. When all matters have been taken care of, the probate administration will be closed and the personal representative relieved of liability. This process often takes one year and sometimes several years, depending upon complexities in the sale of assets, the payments of bills and taxes, and disputes among heirs.

One of the common complaints concerning the probate process is the **minimum fees** the statute allows to the personal representative and the attorney. These fees have long been established and are structured on a sliding scale ending at two percent on all estate assets over $1 million dollars.

Based upon the time, expenses, and public exposure of the probate process, most people choose another avenue to manage and transfer their estates in order to avoid the probate process.

DURABLE POWER OF ATTORNEY

Q & A

Question 1: When can a person sign documents or make financial decisions for someone else?
Answer: Only when a person has been designated under a Durable Power of Attorney (DPOA) as an agent or attorney-in-fact with authority currently vested. (Or if appointed by the court as conservator)

Question 2: How must a person act when carrying out his or her duties under a DPOA?
Answer: An attorney-in-fact is a fiduciary, which requires that person to act under a standard of care even higher than the standard that would be used in managing his or her own property. Fiduciaries have legal duties to the person for whom they are acting.

Question 3: What powers does a person have when working under a DPOA?
Answer: The power granted under the power of attorney document is the power given to the agent/attorney-in-fact.

Question 4: Does a DPOA give the agent/attorney-in-fact the ability to act at any time?
Answer: If the DPOA is springing, then the agent/attorney-in-fact may only act after the principal is determined to be incapacitated. A DPOA also terminates at death.

In many instances, the management of one's estate during life is more important than how the estate is managed at death. Accordingly, the designation of an agent or attorney-in-fact under a power of attorney is vitally important. Like any other appointment or delegation of power, the appointee must be trustworthy.

Each state has its own power of attorney laws, e.g., R.S.Mo. Sections 404.700-737. The principal is the person who has created a power of attorney. Under the statute, an **attorney-in-fact** is any individual or corporation appointed to act as the agent of a principal in a written power of attorney. The law provides for successor attorneys-in-fact to be designated in the event that an agent becomes incapacitated, resigns, or dies. The principal may appoint multiple attorneys-in-fact who may be designated to act jointly or individually.

A "**durable**" power of attorney is a written power of attorney that does not terminate in the event of the principal becoming disabled or incapacitated. This type of power of attorney generally continues until the principal dies. In order to qualify as a durable power of attorney, the law requires that certain and precise language be inserted into the document. A durable power of attorney does not have to be recorded in order for it to be effective; however, if the power of attorney is used for real estate transactions, the recording of the instrument will be required in order to establish a clear succession of title.

The power of attorney may grant **general powers** to the attorney-in-fact under the statute R.S.Mo. Section 404.710 or delineate specific powers in detail. A thorough instrument should cover every power contemplated to be necessary to carry out the principal's affairs. This would include changing financial accounts, making gifts, designating beneficiaries on insurance contracts, retirement accounts, and all other non-probate transfers, and creating and amending revocable trust agreements.

All of the actions of an attorney-in-fact must be exercised as a fiduciary, which implies that the standard of conduct is higher than if the principal was making decisions for himself or herself. This means that the attorney-in-fact has a **fiduciary obligation** to exercise the powers conferred in the best interests of the principal and to avoid self-dealing and conflicts of interest. An attorney-in-fact must maintain accounts and interests in a manner that clearly indicates his or her capacity and keep these accounts separate from all others, including the personal acts of the attorney-in-fact.

There are **specific powers** that the law requires to be set forth in the instrument in order to utilize them. For example, the power of attorney must specifically state that the attorney-in-fact may (1) amend or execute a trust, (2) fund a trust, (3) make or revoke a gift, (4) disclaim a gift, (5) create or change survivorship interests, (6) designate or change a beneficiary, (7) give consent to an autopsy, (8) make an anatomical gift, (9) give consent to medical treatment, and (10) designate successor agents. If not specifically stated, these items cannot be done by the attorney-in-fact. On the other hand, no power of attorney may create or modify a will, make or modify a living will, force a principal to take any type of action, or carry out any action specifically forbidden by the principal.

An attorney-in-fact may be given notification in an instrument that the authority granted cannot be exercised until the happening of an event, condition, or contingency. Missouri law allows a power of attorney to only be activated upon the disability of the principal if so stated in the document. Based upon a physician's statement or court determination, the attorney-in fact's authority "**springs**" into existence. This is commonly known as a springing power of attorney and is distinguished from a "**vested**" power of attorney, which grants immediate authority to the attorney-in-fact when the instrument is signed by the principal.

A power of attorney may be **modified or terminated** orally or in writing; however, prudence would dictate that a written instrument always be used in order to substantiate the act taken. The terms and conditions set forth in the power of attorney instrument may dictate precisely how the instrument may be modified or amended.

A power of attorney may be terminated in several ways, including by the terms of the instrument, on the filing of a divorce of the principal and the attorney-in-fact, and upon the death of the principal. Upon the death of the principal, the power of attorney ends, except for the limited purposes of carrying out the power to request an autopsy or to make an anatomical gift. The attorney-in-fact should be notified in the event a power of attorney is terminated so that the attorney-in-fact is aware that his or her authority is terminated.

Third parties dealing with the attorney-in-fact who are acting in good faith may rely upon the power of attorney instrument without inquiring into the authenticity of a certified copy, the validity of the designation or qualification of the attorney-in-fact, the propriety of the actions taken, the disability or incapacity of the principal, or whether or not the authority has been modified or terminated.

The power of attorney may also provide for the attorney-in-fact to **delegate** any or all of the powers granted under the instrument. This delegation must, however, be subject to the attorney-in-fact's directions or limitations. Accordingly, an attorney-in-fact may delegate investment or tax decisions to a qualified financial advisor or accountant.

An attorney-in-fact may receive reasonable **compensation** for services rendered to the principal in accordance with the provisions granted under the instrument. This compensation may be computed on a reasonable hourly rate or as otherwise set forth in the power of attorney.

In all events, the principal, the principal's representative, or the principal's creditors may petition the court for an **accounting** by the attorney-in-fact in order to review and approve all of the transactions made and actions taken by him or her. The court may order the attorney-in-fact to exercise or refrain from exercising a power in a particular manner for a particular purpose, modify the authority granted under the instrument, suspend the power, terminate the power, remove the attorney-in-fact, confirm the authority, or issue any other order deemed to be in the best interest of the principal.

A durable power of attorney is a powerful instrument that should be able to fix most problems that may arise while the principal is living. This type of power grants the attorney-in-fact the authority to act as if he or she and the principal were one and the same. The power of attorney should be created to work in concert with the principal's other estate planning documents when contemplating all reasonable contingencies, and may be specific or limited in nature.

TRANSFERS TO MINORS

Q & A

Question 1: Who holds the funds for a minor under the Missouri Transfers to Minors Law?
Answer: A custodian holds the funds for a minor and may use the funds for the minor's health, education, maintenance, and support.

Question 2: When must the funds be surrendered to the minor?
Answer: Generally, at age 21.

Missouri, like most states, has repealed the old uniform gifts to minors law and replaced it with the Missouri Transfers to Minors Law, i.e., R.S.Mo. Sections 404.007-094. Under these statutes, property may be transferred to a person who is a minor on the date of the transfer by the transference of the property to a custodian for the benefit of the minor. For the purposes of this law in Missouri, a minor is an individual who has not reached the age of 21.

A **donor** making a transfer of property may designate funds to be held in a minor's account during life under a will, trust, deed, insurance contract, annuity, or by a non-probate transfer. When the property is received or an account has been created, the interest should be designated "as **custodian** for...under the Missouri Transfers to Minors Law."

Once the property interest or account has been established, the custodian may deliver, pay over, or expend for the minor's benefit income or principal necessary for the support of the minor. This would include health, education, and maintenance of the minor. However, this does not affect the obligation of any person, including the minor's parent, to **support** the minor.

To the extent that the custodial property has not been expended, the custodian must deliver the property (1) to the minor upon him or her reaching age **21** or reaching age 18 upon the minor's request (for property created by a transfer from a person other than a donor), or (2) to the minor's probate estate upon the minor's death. If the custodian does not deliver the property to the minor or the minor's estate, the minor or the minor's personal representative may petition the court to deliver the property as required under the law.

While the custodian is holding the property for the minor, the property may be deposited or invested with financial institutions or brokers as deemed proper by the custodian. A minor who has reached the age of **14**, or the minor's representative, may at any time **petition** the court for an accounting by the custodian as to the investments and transactions made on behalf of the minor.

At all times, the custodian must maintain records of all transactions with respect to the custodial property, including information necessary for the preparation of the minor's tax returns. For services rendered on behalf of the minor, the custodian may elect to receive from the custodial property reasonable compensation for each calendar year.

In the event that a custodian cannot act, dies, or resigns, the law provides for a **successor** to be nominated by a person with a power from the donor, the custodian, or the custodian's legal representative. If a successor custodian has not been designated, a minor over the age of 14, a guardian, an adult member of the minor's family, or any person interested in the welfare of the minor may petition the court to designate a successor custodian. If allowed upon the creation of the account or document, the donor should designate successor custodians in the event the initial custodian is unable to act.

Although the law provides for the transfer to minors, the requirement that the property be tendered to the minor at age 21 is often cause for regret for the donor of the property. In many cases, the donor would have desired that the funds be held for the individual's benefit for a longer period and may have intended that the funds be used for a specific purpose. As a result of the donor's desire to customize the manner in which an individual may receive assets, most clients prefer the creation and use of a trust for the benefit of minors and other loved ones.

TRUSTS

Q & A

Question 1: Must a trust be a written document?
Answer: No, but a written agreement will clearly set forth the terms and conditions of all relevant matters.

Question 2: When can a trust be established?
Answer: A trust may be created under a person's will (and thus only is effective after death) or may be created during his or her lifetime.

Question 3: Who has a right to know of a trust's existence?
Answer: The current income beneficiaries, as well as the future qualified beneficiaries, have a right to know about the trust after it has become irrevocable.

Question 4: Once a trust has become irrevocable, can it be changed?
Answer: Generally, no, but a post-2005 trust may be amended with the approval of the settlor and beneficiaries. In addition, the court always retains the power to amend a trust if necessary.

Question 5: May creditors attach the assets of a trust?
Answer: That depends upon whether the trust is a discretionary trust, whether the trust has a spendthrift provision, and whether the settlor has retained power over the trust.

Question 6: Can a trust be contested?
Answer: Yes, but the procedure to contest a trust is complicated and may require multiple lawsuits and can also potentially impact a beneficiary's interest in a trust.

Question 7: What are the duties of a trustee?
Answer: The trustee must carry out the terms and conditions set forth under the trust agreement and will be liable for breach of trust if the duties are not fulfilled. A court may order a trustee to give an accounting of the trust administration and may replace a trustee.

Question 8: How is a trust taxed?
Answer: That depends on whether the trust is a "grantor" trust under the IRC. Generally, while the settlor is living, the settlor will be taxed if the trust is revocable by him or her. Usually, when the trust becomes irrevocable, e.g., at the death of a settlor, the trust will file its own tax return and pay its own taxes.

For thousands of years, individuals have been able to enter into trust agreements in order to manage and distribute property interests for the benefit of other individuals or themselves. These **equitable arrangements** have taken many forms and have been used in a variety of circumstances.

Trust agreements can be either oral or **written agreements**. All creations of trust composed of lands and property interests must be proved by some writing signed by the creator. These agreements are created by a settlor or grantor, are managed by a trustee or administrator, and are held or distributed for the benefit of individual(s) known as beneficiaries. Under modern legal theory, an individual may be the settlor, trustee, and beneficiary simultaneously. Technically, a trust includes any express, private, charitable, constructive, or any other type of trust determined by a court's decree. The MUTC sets forth the laws of trusts under R.S.Mo. Sections 456.001 to 456.11-1106.

A trust may be **created** by a transfer of property, which is the declaration that property is held in trust for a beneficiary or can be created by court order. Any person who has the capacity to create a trust may create a trust if (1) a clear intention is expressed for any lawful purpose including charitable purposes, (2) definite beneficiaries are indicated or can be ascertained, and (3) the trustee is granted duties. A trust may be created under a will, which is commonly known as a testamentary trust.

In order for an individual to be able to establish a trust, he or she must have the **testamentary capacity** necessary to establish a will. Therefore, the settlor must be of "sound and disposing mind and memory." This standard is met when the person signing the trust (1) is able to understand the ordinary affairs of life, (2) is able to understand the nature and extent of his or her property, (3) is able to know the natural objects of his or her bounty, and (4) can intelligently weigh and appreciate his or her natural obligations to those persons.

The Missouri statutes grant broad powers to the settlor in creating a trust agreement. Trusts may be created for all types of beneficiaries and for varied **purposes**, including the creation of trusts for animals. The terms and conditions of a trust may be customized to fit any circumstance that is lawful and not against public policy.

Once a trust has been established, it is normally kept safe and is a private document known only to the settlor, trustee, and beneficiaries. Although a trust can be **registered** with the local probate court, most trusts are never registered. In the event that a court determination is sought regarding a trust arrangement, a trust may be registered, and the trustee will thereby submit themselves to the personal jurisdiction of the court.

In most cases, a revocable trust is **amendable** by the settlor until his or her death is proven by an authenticated copy of a death certificate or until a person is proven to be absent for a continuous period of five years after a diligent search. In most cases, the death of the settlor is the triggering event that subjects the trust property to administration and/or distribution to the remainder beneficiaries.

All trust distributions are subject to the trustee being able to locate the beneficiaries and the beneficiaries being able to claim their distributions. The law has incorporated procedures for **unclaimed** trust property. In the event that trust property cannot be distributed, the court always retains the authority to deviate from the trust terms and order a distribution to fulfill the purposes of the trust.

There are different **types of beneficiaries** under a trust that are distinguished from each other based upon each beneficiary's right to currently receive distributions of income or principal (permissible distributee) and those who would receive a distribution if the rights of the permissible distributee expired or the trust terminated (qualified beneficiary).

In most cases, the trust will administer and distribute trust property in accordance with the **terms and conditions** contained under the trust instrument. Under the Missouri statutes, the terms of a trust will generally prevail over any other provisions of the law. There are, however, certain terms that any trust instrument may not contain. For example, a trust may not (1) alter the statutory requirements for creating a trust; (2) change the trustee's duty to act in good faith; (3) circumvent the requirement to benefit the beneficiaries; (4) alter the court's power to modify a trust, require a bond, adjust compensation, or exercise justice; (5) alter the duty of a trustee to notify each permissible distributee, respond to a qualified beneficiary's request for information, or change the trustee's liability to a beneficiary; (6)

alter the effect of spendthrift provision; or (7) alter the periods for filing a lawsuit against the trustee.

In order for a trust to establish a sufficient connection with a legal jurisdiction, trust terms may designate a **place of administration**. This place may be altered or transferred as circumstances change. If a settlor believes a particular jurisdiction grants an advantageous tax status or creditor protection, the place of administration may be altered after proper notice has been given to the beneficiaries.

The question of who is entitled to receive **notices** concerning the trust or its administration is important and is set forth in detail under R.S.Mo. Section 456.8-813. Notice is generally to be given to those persons who will be affected by a distribution or action taken by a trustee. Notice to a person who may represent and bind another person has the same effect as if the notice were given directly to the other person.

The trustee has a **duty to inform each qualified beneficiary** of any material fact that may affect each beneficiary's interests and shall promptly reply to a beneficiary's request for information. A trustee, upon the request of a beneficiary, must furnish a copy of the trust instrument within 180 days (formerly 60 days) of accepting trusteeship, or of the trust becomes irrevocable. The beneficiary must also be given certain information about the trustee, including the rate of compensation.

In addition to other notices, the permissible distributees must be given a **trustee's report** annually. This report does not have to be rendered in any particular form but must communicate the liabilities, receipts, and disbursements, e.g., a financial institution's statement or a bank account record.

Generally, the **consent** of a person who may represent another person or appoint beneficial interests is binding on the person represented. A minor, incapacitated, or unborn individual, or a person whose identity or location is unknown, may be represented and bound by another person having a substantially identical interest with respect to a particular question or dispute. This concept is commonly known as "**virtual representation**." As long as there is no conflict, a guardian, parent, agent, conservator, trustee, or personal representative may represent, give consent, and bind a beneficiary. If the representation is ever deemed to be inadequate, the court may appoint a representative for any individual.

A trust will continue as long as the document indicates in order to fulfill its purposes. Generally, a trust continues until it is **revoked**, expires pursuant to its terms, accomplishes all its purposes, or until it is impossible to achieve. As between a husband and wife, a trust will be revoked with regard to any property interest in favor of the settlor's former spouse if the settlor's marriage is dissolved or annulled. In this case, the terms of the trust shall be given effect as if the former spouse had died immediately before the date of the dissolution. In this case, prudence would dictate that a trust be reviewed and properly amended.

With regard to a revocable trust, the settlor retains the power to **terminate the trust** at any time. Normally, once a settlor has died, the trust becomes irrevocable and may then only be terminated by its own terms, the court, or by the beneficiaries with the court's approval. The law will allow an **irrevocable trust to be modified or terminated** without court approval upon the consent of the settlor and all beneficiaries. If all of the beneficiaries do not consent, the court could modify or terminate a trust if it finds that the interests of all the beneficiaries who do not consent are adequately protected. In the event that the settlor does not consent or is not living, the law allows the adult beneficiaries to consent to a modification or termination of a trust if the court finds that the interests of any nonconsenting beneficiary will be adequately protected. These procedures for modifying or terminating a trust are applicable to trusts that became irrevocable after January 1, 2005, pursuant to R.S.Mo. Sections 456.4A-411 and 456.4B-411.

With regard to **charitable trusts**, there are different procedures for modifying and terminating the terms of such a trust. In this case, if the trust becomes unlawful, impracticable, impossible to achieve, or wasteful, the court may apply the "cy pres" doctrine and direct that the trust property be applied or distributed in a manner consistent with the settlor's charitable intent.

In the event that a trust has a value of less than $100,000 and is insufficient to justify the cost of administration, the trustee may terminate the trust. The determination of whether a trust has become **uneconomical** is made by the trustee after the beneficiaries have been given notice of the same.

Upon termination of a trust, the trustee shall distribute all of the property as directed by the trust instrument or by the court. As is the case with a **trust distribution**, when a trust is terminated, a settlement should be given by the trustee in order to substantiate the distribution and allow the beneficiaries to examine the propriety of the disposition.

In many instances, either the trustee or the beneficiaries may wish to **reform the trust** instrument without terminating it. Accordingly, the court may reform an irrevocable trust to correct mistakes if there is clear evidence that the settlor's intent was affected by a mistake of fact or law. A court may also reform an irrevocable trust to achieve the settlor's tax objectives.

In the event that the trustee sees a need to **combine** two or more trusts or to **divide** a trust into two or more trusts, the trustee may do so if the action will not impair the rights of the beneficiaries or adversely affect the purposes of the trust.

Once a trust has been established, the issue of **creditor attachment** of trust assets is important and must be examined. The right of creditors to attach assets of a trust depends upon many factors, including whether the trust is revocable by the settlor, subject to a spendthrift provision, or whether the beneficiary has a right to a present or future distribution.

Generally, the property of a revocable trust is subject to the claims of the settlor's **creditors**, because the settlor can obtain his or her property at any time without restriction. Missouri law does allow a **self-settled trust** to be free from creditor attachment under R.S.Mo. Section 456.5-505 if the trust is (1) irrevocable; (2) the settlor is not the sole beneficiary of either the income or the principal; (3) the settlor does not retain the power to amend the trust, or the settlor is one of a class of beneficiaries and does not retain the right to receive a specific portion of income or principal that is determined solely from the provisions of the trust instrument; and (4) the conveyance of assets to the trust was not fraudulent as to creditors.

A **spendthrift clause** can be inserted into a trust document and is valid to restrain either or both the voluntary or involuntary transfer of a beneficiary's interest. This term has been commonly used to protect a beneficiary who is a spendthrift from his or her creditors with regard to property held in trust for that person's benefit. As a matter of public policy, even if a trust has a spendthrift provision, a beneficiary's child, spouse, or former spouse who has a judgment against the beneficiary for support or maintenance may obtain an order from the court to attach present or future trust income. The spendthrift clause does not, however, protect the settlor

A beneficiary's right under a trust will not be subject to **creditors** if the interest is subject to the **trustee's discretion**. This is true even though the discretion to distribute is expressed in the form of a standard, such as health, education, maintenance, and support. Under this discretionary standard, the trust property does not constitute an interest that a creditor or claimant may attach. In this situation, the beneficiary may also serve as a trustee or co-trustee. This protection will apply to a beneficiary's interest regardless of the application of a spendthrift provision. As long as the distribution to the beneficiary is not required to be made by the trustee, the discretion of the trustee will prevent creditors from attaching the trust assets.

A settlor's **creditor's rights** to attach trust assets will also be terminated after the settlor's death if the trustee **publishes notice** in a newspaper for four consecutive weeks declaring that the trustee will pay all debts that are submitted to him or her within six months. After this six-month period has expired, all creditors against the trust are forever barred from making claims and attaching trust assets.

The majority of individuals use a **revocable living trust** as a will substitute. Under the terms of such a trust, the settlor may revoke or amend the instrument and may freely withdraw trust assets. If the terms of the trust provide for a method of revoking or amending the trust, the trust may be revoked or amended by substantially complying with those terms. If no terms for revocation or amendment are given, then the settlor may revoke or amend the trust by manifesting clear and convincing evidence of his or her intent. Because of the technical requirements of the trust code and the rules of evidence, all trust revocations and amendments should be accomplished with the assistance of legal counsel and should be in writing.

The settlor will retain the right to revoke and amend the trust until he or she has been deemed totally **incapacitated**. This determination may be made by a court but is usually made by a licensed physician who has given an affidavit or letter of incapacity. After the settlor has been deemed incapacitated, the successor trustees designated under the trust instrument may take over the administration of the trust upon their acceptance of the same.

After a trust has been established and the settlor has died, a person may commence a judicial proceeding to **contest the trust** within the earlier of (1) two years of the settlor's death or (2) six months after the trustee has sent the person a copy of the trust, informed him or her of the trustee, and stated the time allowed for the contest. If the trust receives assets from the settlor's will, the time to contest the trust is shortened to the six-month period for contesting the will (but only if the trust has been filed with the probate court within 90 days of the first probate publication). After a settlor has died and claims have been addressed, the trustee may begin to distribute trust assets without liability, unless he or she knows of a pending trust contest or if a potential contestant has notified the trustee.

Although the law sets forth a method for **contesting a trust**, it is an arduous task to prove that the settlor was not competent when he or she executed the instrument or was somehow coerced into constructing the document in a certain way. If the trust is somehow broken and the assets are free of trust, the question remains of how the assets should then be distributed. In this case, the non-probate law allows certain persons to reach out and recover certain transfers made by the decedent during his or her life. Such an action must be taken within 16 months of the decedent's death.

Although the probate code and the Non-Probate Transfer Act provide for statutory shares for a spouse and children, the trust law does not. Therefore, the assets of the probate estate must be insufficient to cover the allowances and claims made against the estate before the trust assets can be applied against them. This, in turn, requires a probate estate to be opened within the statutory time limits. After this has been done, an action for accounting must be filed seeking to **recover the trust assets** into the probate estate which are then to be recovered under the non-probate law. In order for this to be done, the personal representative, creditor, spouse, or child who is known as a "qualified claimant," must bring such an action within the probate estate. This is accomplished by the qualified claimant delivering a written demand upon the personal representative within 30 days; the action may then commence. In this case, the personal representative must allege in a petition that he or she is the recipient of the recoverable transfers, i.e., the trust. All of this may be a moot point if the trustee had published notice of the six-month period to bring claims against the trust estate. If a judgment is granted under this confusing procedure, only a proportionate amount of the value of the trust assets may be recovered from each beneficiary as a monetary judgment. If the assets are squandered, there may be no money to recover, since no lien of any kind is authorized under the statute. In conclusion, breaking a trust and recovering its assets into the probate estate is a very complex and challenging task.

Once a trust instrument has been executed, the person designated as the trustee may **accept trusteeship** by complying with terms of the trust or by accepting delivery of the trust property. Any person designated as a trustee may decline to serve as such within a reasonable period after becoming aware of his or her designation. In any event, a designated trustee may inspect or act to preserve the property without accepting trusteeship.

A trust may nominate and designate trustees to act simultaneously as **co-trustees**. Additionally, a well-drafted trust instrument will set forth successor trustees to act in the event that any predecessor trustee dies, becomes incapacitated, or resigns. In this situation, each trustee has the obligation to prevent a co-trustee from committing a breach of trust and to redress such a breach.

A trustee may **delegate** to an agent (e.g., a financial advisor) duties and powers that are proper and must establish the scope and terms of the delegation. In any event, a trustee may dissent from the actions taken by the majority of the other trustees or actions taken by a delegated agent. In the event that a trustee no longer desires to serve under the trust, he or she may resign upon giving at least 30 days' notice to the qualified beneficiaries. All resignations should be accompanied by a settlement of the trust affairs given to the beneficiaries and successor trustee.

The settlor, a trustee, or a qualified beneficiary may request the court to **remove a trustee**. A trustee may be removed if the court determines that (1) the trustee committed a serious breach, (2) there was a lack of cooperation among the trustees that substantially impaired the trust administration, or (3) the trustee is proven to be unfit, unwilling, or continually fails to administer the trust properly. A corporate trustee may be removed if it is proven that it has substantially reduced the level of services provided to the trust within 90 days after receiving notice of the failure.

If a **breach of trust** has occurred, a beneficiary may commence an action within one year of (1) a report that adequately discloses the potential claim and (2) the date that the trustee informed the beneficiary of the time limits to proceed with a potential claim. In any event, a proceeding for breach of trust must be commenced within five years of (1) the removal, resignation, or death of the trustee; (2) the termination of the beneficiary's interest; or (3) the termination of the trust.

The terms of a trust may grant relief from liability to a trustee. Those terms, however, will only be enforced if the trustee did not act in bad faith and did not abuse the relationship with the settlor. These terms of limited liability are commonly known as **exculpatory clauses**. In all instances, these clauses must be fair under the circumstances and may not protect actions made in bad faith or reckless indifference. A beneficiary may always **release a trustee from liability**, as long as the release was not induced by improper conduct and the beneficiary knew of his or her rights regarding the breach.

Most trust instruments will circumvent the requirement to obtain a **bond** insuring the trust assets. Nevertheless, a trustee will need to protect the trust assets as a reasonable fiduciary and prudent investor. In carrying out his or her duties, the trustee may be reimbursed for expenses and advances he or she incurred in the administration of the trust. A trustee also receives reasonable **compensation** as directed under the trust instrument. The court may allow additional compensation if it is proven that the trustee's duties were substantially different from those originally contemplated. A normal trustee fee would be based upon one percent of the value of the trust or a percentage of income and principal equaling roughly the same amount, and the fee is usually paid annually. Both trustee reimbursement and compensation may be made out of the trust property.

A well-drafted trust instrument will refer to the **powers** granted to a trustee under the state statutes and will delineate specific powers that the settlor believes will be necessary to carry out the trust purposes. An individual never knows to what extent a trust may be funded. All types of assets may be acquired during life through work, gift, chance, or otherwise. Accordingly, the trust powers should include, at a minumum, the ability to hold and manage real estate, bank accounts, stock portfolios, tangible property, insurance, retirement accounts, corporations, limited liability companies, partnerships, and mineral rights, as well as the ability to transfer gifts and manage assets of all kinds. A trust may be the recipient of properties not previously contemplated or may acquire assets through exchange. The conclusion is to draft the powers clause to be broad as possible without adversely affecting any tax traps.

As a general precept, a trustee must administer the trust solely in the interests of the beneficiaries and must maintain the trust assets in a manner that serves their interests. All of the trustee's transactions must be free from any **personal conflicts** and should never involve an action that may result in the trustee taking advantage of a beneficiary.

If there are multiple beneficiaries, the trustee must **deal impartially** in managing and distributing the property, giving due regard to the beneficiaries' respective interests. The trustee shall, therefore, exercise its powers with reasonable care, skill, and caution. If a trustee has special skills or expertise, he or she must use those skills or expertise.

While a trust is revocable, the trustee may follow a **direction from the settlor** that is contrary to the terms of the trust. The terms of the trust may confer upon a trustee or other person a power to direct the modification or termination of the trust. In this instance, the person exercising the power is considered a fiduciary required to act in good faith.

In all instances, the trustee must **protect** the trust property, which may mean that the property should be insured. Additionally, the trustee is obligated to maintain adequate **records** regarding the trust assets and all transactions, which may mean that the respective interests of each beneficiary must be clearly designated.

As an alternative to providing a full copy of the trust, third parties and other persons dealing with the trustee may request that a **trust certification** be given verifying that the trust is in force. This certification must contain certain information concerning the settlor, trustee, trustee power, and revocability of the trust. The certification must be signed by the trustee but does not need to contain all of the dispositive provisions of the trust.

The trustee has a duty to **invest** the trust assets pursuant to the Missouri Prudent Investor Act, unless the settlor has expanded or restricted the rule. Under the act, the trustee must consider the purposes, terms, and distribution requirements of the trust. A trustee's investment and management must be evaluated, not in isolation, but in the context of the trust portfolio as a whole and as a part of an overall investment strategy having risk and return objectives reasonably suited to the trust. The trustee must consider (1) the economic conditions, (2) inflation and deflation, (3) legal consequences, (4) the need for cash, (5) the total return from investments, (6) other resources of the beneficiary, (7) the need for liquidity, (8) a specific asset's special relationship, (9) the size of the portfolio, and (10) any special skills the trustee or an agent may possess. A trustee has the general duty to diversify trust investments and must periodically review the investment plan. Additionally, the trustee must only incur costs that are appropriate and reasonable.

The trustee also has the duty to allocate receipts and disbursements to or between income and principal for tax and distribution purposes. This allocation is subject to the terms of the trust and the powers granted thereunder. The law grants the trustee the power to adjust **income and principal** in a consistent manner. In making an adjustment, the trustee must consider (1) the purpose and duration of the trust, (2) the settlor's intent, (3) the circumstances of the beneficiaries, (4) the need for liquidity, (5) the trust assets, (6) the increase or decrease of the value of the trust, (7) the power to invade principal, and (8) the general economic conditions. The law also allows for a trustee to convert a trust distribution into a unitrust payment. Under a unitrust payment, between three and five percent of the trust value can be distributed annually. This type of payment results in a uniform payment each year.

Because most individuals desire their estate plans to be private and to avoid the probate system, **living trusts** have become the estate planning vehicle of choice. Due to the complexity of issues, a trust should only be drafted by a licensed attorney who understands the field of law concerning trusts and estates. Once the documents have been created, it is important to remember that unless (1) the estate assets are titled in the name of the trust, (2) the trust is the designated beneficiary of the assets, or (3) the will pours over the assets into the trust, the trustee will have no **authority to dispose of the assets**.

If a trust has been properly constructed and the estate assets have been titled into the trust, then those assets will be **managed** through the trust without court involvement for the lifetime of the settlor, avoiding guardianship and conservatorship proceedings. If the settlor cannot act, the successor trustee will take over the trust administration. Depending upon the family dynamics and the complexity of the estate assets, it may be desirable to nominate a **corporate trustee** to administer the trust. A corporate trustee will ensure that the trust is administered in a professional and impartial manner without feeling pressure from family members.

During the lifetime of the settlor of a revocable living trust, the **settlor's social security number** is used to report trust income. Because such a trust is classified as a "**grantor trust**" under the Internal Revenue Code (IRC), the trust income is reported on the settlor's personal 1040 income tax return without the necessity of obtaining a separate tax identification number. When the settlor is no longer the trustee, and upon the trust becoming irrevocable (at the settlor's death), a **separate tax identification number** must be obtained and all taxable events reported under that number.

In any event, if a trust has been properly drafted and funded, the estate assets should be distributed without the necessity of a probate administration. In most cases, the surviving spouse will be taken care of, and the surviving children will inherit the residue upon the surviving spouse's death. During the life of the surviving spouse and/or children, the trustee can be directed to support them in accordance with their standard of living for their health, education, and maintenance. A settlor has control over how to dispose of his or her estate; for example, sub-trusts can be established for children that would support them until a certain age, after which their respective inheritances can be distributed over time in a variety of methods.

If it is advantageous to establish sub-trusts to segregate funds for tax purposes, the settlor can establish these trusts when the trust is initially drafted.

A properly constructed estate plan will integrate the trust, durable power of attorney, and last will and testament so that they work in conjunction with each other. Typically, the settlor retains full **control** over the trust during his or her lifetime. After the settlor's death or incapacity, the trust management continues through a successor. Pursuant to the terms and conditions contained in the trust instrument, the assets are held or distributed for the benefit of a spouse, children, or other beneficiaries, and, at the appropriate time, the trust is terminated.

Top 10 Planning Tips – Estate Fundamentals

1. If a person has children under age 18, a **guardian** must be named under that person's last will and testament.
2. **Joint ownership** of property should be reviewed carefully, paying particular attention to who may access the property and whose creditors may attach the property, as well as who will eventually retain possession of the property at the death of an owner.
3. In estates of all sizes, **beneficiary designations** should be carefully implemented by adding POD or TOD to the titles of assets. This designation will override the designations under a will, but it will not be as thorough as may be set forth under a trust instrument.
4. In order to administer a will, the will must be **probated** through the court.
5. A **personal representative**/executor must be appointed in all probate administrations with assets exceeding $40,000 in value. Both the attorney and the personal representative may receive a statutory fee based upon the value of the probate estate.
6. In order to have someone else sign documents and mange one's financial affairs during an individual's life, a **durable power of attorney** must be signed by the principal.

7. A durable power of attorney should set forth detailed powers, name backup agents, and clearly define when and how the powers are to be implemented.
8. Assets for minors may be held in a Missouri **transfers to minors account** and managed by a custodian until a minor reaches age 21.
9. In order to manage and distribute a moderate or large estate outside of the probate system with a detailed dispositive plan, a **revocable living trust** is generally the best estate planning tool.
10. A revocable living trust is a **flexible document** that can set forth beneficiary designations in detail, take advantage of tax planning, and avoid probate.

CHAPTER TWO – ESTATE MANAGEMENT

An estate plan is only as good as the management and distribution that is accomplished when an individual is in need. A person must make sufficient plans to cover (1) medical treatments or emergencies; (2) financial transactions and distributions, including the payment of taxes; and (3) care of children and other loved ones.

HEALTH CARE DIRECTIVES AND HIPAA

Q & A

Question 1: What must a person do to give someone **authority to make medical decisions** for him or her during incapacity?
Answer: A health care directive (HCD) must be signed designating a health care agent and setting forth the powers and duties the agent is to receive.

Question 2: Can a health care directive grant the power to release **medical records**?
Answer: Yes. If the HCD contains a HIPAA release, the agent may access medical records.

Question 3: Can an HCD authorize someone to withdraw and release **life-sustaining treatment**?
Answer: Yes. The law allows a person to authorize another person to release or withdraw death-prolonging procedures.

Most states have established laws concerning an individual's right to declare his or her intention concerning **medical treatment** and death-prolonging procedures. The Nancy Cruzan case was filed in Missouri and was ruled upon by the US Supreme Court establishing a citizen's right to make a written declaration concerning his or her medical treatment when that individual has a terminal condition or fatal pathology.

Under the law (R.S.Mo. Sections 459.010-055), an individual who has reached the age of **18** may sign a declaration regarding his or her health care. Under the statute, a **death-prolonging procedure** is a procedure which, when applied to a patient, would only serve to artificially prolong the dying process and where, in the judgment of the attending physician, death will occur within a short time regardless of any procedure being implemented. A **terminal condition** is an incurable or irreversible condition which, in the opinion of the attending physician, is such that death will occur within a short time regardless of medical procedures.

Such a declaration must be (1) in writing, (2) signed by the person, (3) dated, and, (4) if not wholly in the declarant's handwriting, signed in the presence of two witnesses. The basic declaration concerning the withholding or withdrawal of a death-prolonging procedure in the event of a terminal condition is known as a "**living will**." This declaration may be revoked at any time and in any manner, as long as the declarant remains competent. The law presumes an individual is competent unless there is actual notice to the contrary, typically an affidavit from a doctor. In all events, when the declarant is able to communicate, that person's directives concerning medical treatment supersede all other declarations.

It is the patient's responsibility to provide notification of the declaration to his or her attending physician. Physicians and health care providers are not liable for relying on a medical declaration if they have acted in good faith pursuant to the declaration.

In addition to the living will statute, Missouri law provides for a "**Durable Power of Attorney for Health Care Act**" (R.S.Mo. Sections 404.800-872). Under this act, an individual may designate a person (called and attorney-in-fact) to act in his or her place for medical purposes. The instruments created under this act are commonly called "**Medical Directives**" or "**Health Care Directives**." The person so appointed is empowered to make medical decisions on behalf of the principal, including **withholding and withdrawing** treatment, specifically **artificially supplied nutrition and hydration**. This authority is based upon the physician (1) first attempting to explain to the patient the intention and consequences of withdrawing or withholding nutrition and hydration, and (2) inserting into the patient's file a certificate that the patient is comatose or unable to understand the explanation.

The attorney-in-fact is obligated to consider information concerning the patient's medical diagnosis. The attorney-in-fact must seek evidence concerning the patient's prognosis and the benefit and burden of the treatment before allowing any preexisting conditions to run their natural courses. The attorney-in-fact's authority begins when two licensed physicians declare the patient incapacitated (unless the document only requires one physician). It is difficult to obtain two independent doctor's opinions.

Health care facilities normally honor medical directives and the decisions of an attorney-in-fact; nevertheless, they are not required to do so if the directives or decisions are contrary to the patient's religious beliefs or the facility's institutional policy. It is unlawful for a health care provider or insurance company to require an individual to execute a medical directive. Once a medical directive has been executed, a copy of it shall be made part of the patient's medical record.

A medical directive may be revoked at any time in any manner that the patient is able to communicate. Once a revocation has occurred, it must be made part of the patient's medical record. Nevertheless, once an attorney-in-fact's authority has been revoked, all third parties and health care providers are absolved of liability, if they rely in good faith upon the instructions of the attorney-in-fact and if they did not have actual notice of the revocation.

A thorough medical directive will incorporate the living will statute and the durable power of attorney for health care as well as the **Health Insurance Portability and Accountability Act of 1996 ("HIPAA")**. Under the HIPAA law, the patient may specifically give consent and authority to disclose any of his or her health information and records to any person or entity so designated. This authority expires one year after the patient's death and may be exercised by the patient's personal representative, if so authorized. For HIPAA purposes, "personal representative" is broadly defined and may include a probate personal representative, trustee, or other persons.

The medical directive should also grant authority to sign contracts, engage medical personnel, grant waivers and releases, consent to a "DNR" order (do not resuscitate), make anatomical gifts, authorize an autopsy, and make funeral arrangements, i.e., the right of sepulcher. The directive should allow for the relief of suffering by the application of pain medicine.

Alternate attorneys-in-fact should be designated in the instrument, and this could include having multiple people acting such as children. A spouse and/or children are often granted the authority to make health care decisions once a physician has determined the patient to be incapacitated. When this has occurred, the attorney-in-fact should carry out the desires of the patient as contained in the medical directive. If multiple agents are appointed, the document should be clear whether unanimous consent or majority rule will apply to decision making.

Finally, the medical directive may spell out precise directives concerning the patient's treatment, including directions concerning personal hygiene and final directions of a personal nature.

AGENTS AND ATTORNEYS-IN-FACT

Q & A

Question 1: What type of person should be **named as an attorney-in-fact**/agent?
Answer: Any individual over the age of 18, who is trustworthy, has common sense, has the ability to organize information, and will seek appropriate counsel could have this responsibility.

In order to properly manage one's estate, it is necessary that specific people be designated to back up an individual's decisions and take control of medical and financial circumstances in an emergency. The first consideration when contemplating the designation of an agent is to be sure that the individual appointed is **trustworthy** and honest. When an individual accepts authority as an agent or attorney-in-fact, that person takes on a **fiduciary obligation** to uphold a standard of care that exceeds the standard the person may use for his or her own assets or health care.

Once an individual is found that can be trusted, an evaluation must be made concerning the individual's capability. It is generally not necessary that an attorney-in-fact have any special skills or knowledge. It is necessary that an individual is able to understand the parameters of his or her authority and have the **common sense** to take care of basic duties such as managing assets and communicating with accountants, attorneys, and financial advisors. Basic duties such as investing funds, filing tax returns, and dealing with personal matters of the principal should be anticipated when deciding on who should be appointed as an agent.

From a practical point of view, an agent should be someone who has the proper personality to work and interact with the principal's family, close friends, and other professionals. If the attorney-in-fact or agent does not have the **temperament** to interact and cooperate with the principal's family and team of professionals, the management of the estate will suffer and most likely waste time and incur fees unnecessarily.

Whenever the principal's professional team can work together in a smooth and efficient manner, the estate will be managed well, and the best interests of the principal will be served.

SUCCESSOR TRUSTEES AND TRUST PROTECTORS

Q & A

Question 1: **Who should be given the authority** to manage an estate?
Answer: Any individual over the age of 18 may be named as a trustee if he or she possesses the honesty, intelligence, and common sense to carry out the duties set forth under the trust instrument. In the event that a conflict arises between the individual trustee and/or beneficiaries, a corporate trustee should be considered. A corporate

trustee will carry out the estate duties impartially, without personal influences affecting them and with knowledge of the estate and tax laws.

Question 2: **How many trustees** should be listed?
Answer: As many backup trustees as is needed may be set forth under the trust instrument.

Question 3: Who will make sure the trustee is **carrying out his or her duties** properly?
Answer: The beneficiaries who receive an accounting can oversee the trustee. A trust protector may also be given the ability to oversee a trustee. In addition, the court always retains jurisdiction to oversee the performance of a trustee.

The same criteria used to pick an attorney-in-fact or agent is the same for choosing a trustee. The trustee must be honest, exhibit common sense, and be able to work with other professionals in an amicable manner. The question of "**who**" will manage an estate is vitally important and should be given due consideration.

Thought should be given to who will succeed a trustee in the event that the first choice is unavailable. Should there be two or more trustees trying to administer the estate simultaneously? Will there be an **emotional or financial conflict** between the trustees or between the trustees and beneficiaries? Should there be an independent trustee who has no vested interest in the estate?

In many instances, there is a need for a professional trust company to administer an estate due to financial, emotional, or practical conflicts. Although an estate administration may be accomplished with the assistance of an attorney, a professional trustee who understands the tax laws, administrative procedures, and is able to manage distributions impartially is sometimes the best choice.

Most **professional trust companies** will charge a similar fee that is customarily based upon a percentage of income and principal accumulation and have a published fee schedule. The level of professional service provided by any established trust company should be consistent, although the level of personal service may vary based upon the size of the estate and the size of the trust company. Most well-drafted documents will allow a majority of the beneficiaries to dismiss a corporate trustee and replace it with another corporate trustee who will work better with the beneficiaries, if necessary.

If an individual who is being considered for trustee nomination is unfamiliar with the management of finances, taxes, or dealing with attorneys and accountants, that person is probably not right for the job.

Most trust instruments will have provisions for an **appointment of a successor trustee** by a previous trustee, the ability to appoint an additional trustee, and allowance for a special, i.e., ancillary, trustee to be appointed for unique trust transactions. Additionally, the trustee will be granted certain powers and be required to adhere to certain responsibilities during the administration of the estate. For example, a trustee will not normally have to acquire a bond insuring his or her performance during the estate's administration. A trustee is not normally liable for tangible personal property which was never in his or her possession. If a trustee has used ordinary diligence and good faith, he or she will normally be exonerated from liability with regard to the sale and investment of trust assets.

A successor trustee will be responsible for the **accounting** of trust assets and will likely be required to report to the beneficiaries on an annual basis. The requirement to report to beneficiaries is often mandated in order to prevent trustee fraud and mismanagement. This gives the beneficiaries the opportunity to police the trustee's administration. A successor trustee will also be required to deal impartially with beneficiaries, file tax returns, and actively manage all investment and cash accounts.

In the event that circumstances have changed over time, trustees are no longer appropriate for the estate administration, beneficiary needs have changed, or unanticipated events have arisen, a **trust protector** can step in to remove and replace a trustee. The trust instrument must appoint a trust protector and grant a trust protector the authority to act and should be carefully drafted in order to grant precise powers that will not be overly broad but still flexible enough to accomplish the settlor's intentions. A trust protector can be viewed as the guardian of the trust and is distinguished from a trustee. The trust protector must act in good faith but is not held to the same fiduciary standard as the trustee. The protector does not carry out the day-to-day administration of the trust but is available to fix problems that may arise. If necessary, the protector may remove and replace a trustee. Additionally, the protector may modify or amend the trust instrument in order to (1) achieve favorable tax status, (2) modify the administrative powers, (3) reflect legal changes, (4) correct errors and ambiguities, (5) correct drafting errors, (6) modify interests of beneficiaries, (7) modify powers of appointment, or (8) change the governing law and situs of the trust. The protector may not, however, add beneficiaries that were not previously provided for under the trust instrument or modify the trust in a way that will create a taxable gift, harm the rights of disabled beneficiaries, or bring assets into the protector's estate. The protector is granted limited rights in order to fix problems that may arise during the administration of the trust which were unforeseen or unanticipated by the settlor. The trust protector may not exercise any power for his or her own personal benefit.

A trustee of a discretionary trust also has the common law ability to **decant a trust**, which means that the trustee retains the power to appoint the trust assets from the trust to another trust unless the original trust prohibits or limits such a power. In this manner, the originating trust or "first trust" can be appointed or "decanted" to a new trust or "second trust." This power is granted to the trustee, and, accordingly, the trustee will continue to be subject to a fiduciary standard of conduct while exercising this power. Under this authority, the trustee may increase the distributions to the beneficiary or remove restrictions the first trust created. Like the trust protector, there are parameters to the trustee's ability to decant and certain actions that are prohibited. For example, the trustee may not reduce a beneficiary's interest if it is subject to a marital deduction, charitable remainder, or annuity payment. The trustee has no duty to decant trust assets but may do so in order to fix problems that may arise during the administration of the trust that were unforeseen or unanticipated by the settlor.

CORPORATIONS, PARTNERSHIPS, AND LIMITED LIABILITY COMPANIES

Q & A

Question 1: How do you **establish** a corporation, limited partnership or limited liability company?
Answer: You must file articles of incorporation or articles of organization with the secretary of state, along with the appropriate filing fee.

Question 2: Where are the **powers, duties, and obligations** of the partners, shareholders, members, managers, officers, and directors found?
Answer: For a corporation, the powers and duties are found in the bylaws and minutes. For limited liability companies and partnerships, the powers and duties are found in the operating agreement or partnership agreement.

Question 3: Where are the shareholder or member **rights toward each other** found?
Answer: For a corporation, by-laws and a restrictive stock/buy-sell agreement sets forth the terms between the shareholders. The close corporations statute provides for a default restrictive stock agreement. For a limited liability company, the operating agreement sets forth the terms between the members. For a partnership, the partnership agreement sets the terms between the partners.

Question 4: How are partnerships, corporations, and limited liability companies **taxed**? Answer: The taxation of an entity depends upon the tax election that the entity has made with the IRS. Most entities may be taxed as a flow-through entity that funnels the net income to the shareholders, members, or partners.

Question 5: Are the assets of a shareholder, member, or limited partner safe from the entity's **creditors**?
Answer: Generally, yes, although the court may pierce the veil of any entity that was used to perpetuate a fraud.

In the event that an individual has undertaken a business interest, it is most often in that person's best interest to run the business within the framework of a **legal entity**. There are many benefits to structuring an entity for business purposes, including (1) liability protection, (2) maintenance of a structure to manage and transfer business interests, and (3) to take advantage of certain tax breaks that an entity may provide.

Corporations may be the most widely known business structure, especially for large businesses. A corporation is a legal entity authorized by state statutes and sanctioned by the secretary of state's office. In the state of the corporation's creation, a corporation is created by preparing articles of incorporation that set forth the entity's purpose as well as its officers and directors. Once the articles have been filed with the secretary of state's office, the proper fee has been paid, and the articles have been approved by the state, the entity is legally created.

After a corporation has been approved and incorporated by the secretary of state's office, **bylaws** must be prepared that spell out the rights and obligations of the officers and directors. The bylaws should set forth the method of notification to shareholders of meetings, the duties of officers, and the details of the corporate financial structure.

In addition to articles and bylaws, a **restrictive stock agreement** should be prepared that spells out the rights and obligations of the shareholders between themselves. These agreements should include arrangements for stock ownership and transfers during life, as well as stock transfers at the death of a shareholder. These agreements should have a buy-sell component that would set forth the terms and conditions for when and to whom stock may be transferred. The agreement may limit who can receive stock, who may maintain voting rights over the management of the corporation, and for what price the stock will be sold. These agreements can be structured as **redemption** agreements between the corporation and the shareholder or a **cross-purchase** agreement between the shareholders themselves. Each type of agreement will have different tax ramifications and must be reviewed with tax counsel. Typically, these agreements are **funded** with an escrow account or insurance proceeds, or arrangements are made for payment to be made pursuant to a promissory note.

One of the primary benefits of establishing a corporation, other than managing the business in an orderly manner, is the **protection it affords from creditors** seizing the assets of an individual shareholder. Generally, a creditor of a corporation may only acquire a judgment against the assets of a corporation regarding business liabilities. This means that a business creditor may not reach the personal assets of an individual shareholder unless the corporate veil is pierced based upon fraud or the failure to maintain basic corporate formalities. This protection is not granted to professionals who have committed malpractice.

In order to properly integrate a corporation into an individual's estate plan, the stock to the corporation must be examined and the **stock certificate titled** in a manner that conforms to the plan. This can be accomplished by many methods, including (1) titling the stock certificate in the name of a trust, (2) designating the stock certificate to be TOD to the intended beneficiary, and (3) redeemed under the buy-sell agreement with the proceeds being directed to the recipient designated under the shareholder's estate plan.

The value of corporate interests, especially **minority interests**, must be taken into account when structuring an estate plan. Income distributions, dividend payments, and transfer values must be analyzed. Careful consideration must be given to who will receive corporate stock and gain the rights to share in the running and profits of the business, as well as who will be able to examine the corporate books and records. A good estate plan will always examine corporate interests and structure a **succession plan** for the corporate interest in accordance with the overall estate plan.

Generally, a corporation is created as a **"C" corporation** subject to taxation as a separate entity from the individual shareholders. The corporation may elect to be taxed as an **"S" corporation** pursuant to IRC Sec. 1361, resulting in the net income of the corporation being deemed, distributed to, and taxed to the shareholders directly. Generally, in order to qualify as an "S" corporation, (1) there must be fewer than 100 shareholders, (2) each shareholder must be a US citizen, and (3) the income of the corporation must be distributed to the shareholders each year.

If the corporation is an "S" corporation, the transfer of shares must be made in accordance with the rules for qualifying **subchapter "S" trusts or electing small business trusts** under IRC Sec. 1361(d) and 1361(e). The "S" stock rules generally state that (1) the stock be segregated by the trustee as a separate share; (2) an election be made for the eligible tax treatment; (3) the separate share must be titled in the name of the current income beneficiary; (4) the share must have only one beneficiary; (5) the trustee must distribute all of the income annually; (6) there is a designation that if the trust is terminated, all of the income and principal will be distributed to the current income beneficiary; and (7) in all instances, the stock will be administered in accordance with the provisions qualifying for a subchapter "S" trust or electing small business trust.

Additionally, the state of Missouri allows the corporation to elect to be treated as a "**close corporation**." Under this election, a corporation of less than 50 shareholders may disregard the formalities of a regular corporation and does not need to keep minutes. The state statute itself sets forth a buy-sell agreement as a default if the shareholders have not entered into a restrictive stock agreement.

If the shareholders of the corporation are professionals, such as doctors, dentists, attorneys, or architects who practice pursuant to a professional code, the corporation may be incorporated as a "**professional corporation**" with the secretary of state. This requires the shareholders to be limited to those persons licensed in a particular profession. This also requires the shareholders to manage the corporation in accordance with the professional rules of conduct promulgated by the profession.

If a corporation is chosen as a business entity, the secretary of state's office will require that an **annual registration** be filed listing the officers, directors, and a registered agent. A small fee must also be paid annually to maintain the corporate charter. If the corporation is dissolved, the assets of the corporation may not be transferred pursuant to the stock ownership, and the probate court will most likely have to transfer the assets at the owner's death.

Partnerships have long been established as joint ventures maintained by two or more persons pursuing a common end. Generally, partnerships do not grant the protection from creditors that corporations do. Each partner is jointly and severably liable for business debts and must receive the partnership profits in accordance with their respective interests. Partnerships may be created by oral agreement, subject to verification by the partners; however, it is always best to create a partnership through proper documentation.

Missouri law allows "**limited partnerships**" to be created wherein the general partner is the only partner subject to liability and has full rights of management. The limited partners are not liable for partnership liabilities and have no rights of management. A limited partnership must be created by a partnership agreement being submitted to the secretary of state.

In most instances, the general partner is a corporation or limited liability company which itself is sheltered from creditor's claims. Although the limited partners may receive pro rata distributions, their involvement with the day-to-day affairs of the enterprise is limited in scope. In most instances, the limited partner is a passive investor who is expecting to share in the investment when the underlying asset is sold, as well as receiving ongoing distributions from the revenue of the partnership.

Limited partnerships are commonly used for real estate ventures when subdividing of realty is impractical and the management is more logically vested in a manager rather than a group of investors. This type of entity works well, since the partnership agreement should set forth the terms and conditions for establishing partner accounts and profit shares. This type of entity works very well for family business interests and, in this situation, is commonly referred to as a **family limited partnership** (FLP).

Limited partnerships do not technically have shares of stock; instead of stock, they issue **units in proportion to the partner's investment**. These units are recorded in the ledger of each partner's capital accounts and represent each partner's ownership interests. Because each partner only owns a piece of the partnership interest, each partner's interest is subject to a **valuation discount** for tax purposes based upon minority rights. Additionally, because the partnership agreement restricts the rights of limited partners from managing the business, liquidating the units, and restricting the persons to whom the interest may be transferred, a valuation discount is granted for tax purposes based upon lack of marketability and liquidity. On the other hand, if partnership interests, especially general partnership interests, are owned, a **valuation premium** may be imputed based upon the right to control, transfer, vote, and liquidate the partnership.

Limited partnerships are commonly used in estate planning in order to hold and manage business interests of all types. As with corporate shares, **partnership units must be titled** correctly to ensure that they are held and eventually distributed in accordance with the partner's estate plan. In order to ensure that the partnership interest will be properly integrated into the partner's estate plan, the **partnership agreement must be analyzed** by legal counsel and modified if necessary.

Over the last 20 years, the use of **limited liability companies** (LLCs) has greatly expanded. Originally, LLCs were a hybrid of the corporate structure and the partnership structure. Over time, LLCs have been sanctioned by most states and, like corporations and partnerships, are entities created by statute. Like corporations, an LLC is created by submitting articles of organization to the secretary of state. Whereas corporations which have bylaws and partnerships have partnership agreements, an LLC must have an operating agreement.

The **operating agreement**, like a partnership agreement and restrictive stock agreement, should set forth the terms and conditions under which the company must act, how the members hold their interests, and how the business profits are distributed. The agreement should include (1) the period in which the company will exist; (2) the name of the company; (3) the members of the company; (4) the interest which each member holds in the company in a capital account; (5) the division of net income to the members; (6) the method of payment of costs, expenses, and liabilities; (7) the managing members' rights and responsibilities; (8) the rights of members to transfer their interests; (9) the rights of the members to redeem each other's interests; and (10) the terms under which the company may be terminated and the assets distributed.

Limited liability companies are commonly used to hold rental properties, farms, real estate investments, and business interests of all kinds. Many of the same rules that apply to partnerships are applicable to LLCs. **Membership units must be titled** correctly to ensure that they are held and eventually distributed in accordance with the member's estate plan. In order to ensure that the membership units will be properly integrated into the member's estate plan, the **operating agreement must be analyzed** by legal counsel and modified if necessary.

Because of the creditor protection afforded a limited liability company and the ease of setting up such an entity, LLCs are being used more often than any other entity for both small and large business ventures. All of the valuation considerations applicable to corporate shares and partnership interests may be available to LLC membership interests if properly structured.

A good estate plan that holds business interests, real estate interests, or joint ventures, should make use of either a corporate, partnership, or limited liability company structure. The use of these entities will ensure centralization of **management,** the organized **transfers** of interests, the **liquidation** of interests, and facilitation of **tax valuation** discounts, if applicable.

ASSET TITLING AND COORDINATION

Q & A

Question 1: How do you **get assets into a trust**?
Answer: You must retitle each asset in the name of the trustee, referencing the trust name and date. This is accomplished by changing the owner of beneficiary designations, depending upon the asset.

Question 2: What **types of assets** should be titled in a living trust?
Answer: Generally, all assets other than retirement accounts, annuities, and other qualified assets should be titled into a living trust, or the trust should be named as the beneficiary of the asset.

Question 3: Should **retirement accounts** be beneficiaried into a living trust?

Answer: Each circumstance must be carefully analyzed before a retirement account is beneficiaried into a trust. The account owner must review the desire and benefit of qualifying a distribution for a spousal rollover or a stretch withdrawal by children or grandchildren. The ability of the beneficiary to receive the retirement benefit must be reviewed. The trust agreement must set forth the terms and conditions of administering a retirement distribution.

In order for an estate to be properly managed and administered, it is vital that the assets be titled properly and that all beneficiary designations have been thought through and completed. In order for a trustee to take control and administer any assets, that particular asset must designate the trustee as the owner or beneficiary of the same. Accordingly, if an asset is not **titled in the name of a trust** or is not paid or transferred to a trust, that asset will be administered through the probate court or as a matter of law by the joint owner, if applicable.

Therefore, when creating a trust, the settlor must be sure to examine each asset and physically change the title or beneficiary designation to the account, deed, or financial instrument. Without changing the title or beneficiary designation, there is no connection between the trust and the assets other than a possible assignment or transfer through the probate court. Accordingly, John Doe must title his assets as "John Doe, Trustee of the John Doe Revocable Living Trust dated January 1, 2011" or "**John Doe Trustee, Doe Trust U/A 1-1-11**." During his life, John Doe will use his Social Security Number as the tax ID number for his revocable living trust.

All **real estate** titles should be changed and deeded into the trust during life by a quit claim deed, general warranty deed, or at death by a beneficiary deed. This means that a deed must be created, signed by the settlor, and filed with the recorder of deeds in the county where the property is located.

All **bank accounts** and certificates of deposit should be retitled and changed into the name of the trust. This must be done at the financial institution that holds the account. As a result, the checks themselves and the account statements will show the trustee as the owner of the account. As an alternative, bank accounts can be paid on death (P.O.D.) to a trust or to certain individuals.

As with the bank accounts, all **investment accounts**, other than retirement accounts and annuities, should be retitled in the trust. Accordingly, these statements will show the trustee as the owner of the portfolio and account. In most cases, when the account has been retitled, all of the stocks, bonds, and other investments in the account are titled in the trust. Individual stocks, bonds, mutual funds, and other investments must be individually retitled into the name of the trust for the trust to have control over them.

All **business interests** must be funneled into the trust by changing the certificate of title (stock certificate or unit), assigning, or making the trust the beneficiary of the interest. Stock certificates may be retitled or beneficiaried into the name of a trust. It should be noted that S corporation stock must comply with all of the criteria set forth under the IRC, and, therefore, any trust that holds S corporation stock must adhere to the regulations for qualifying S corporation trusts. LLC units may be titled or beneficiaried into the name of a trust. Partnership interests may be titled or beneficiaried into the name of a trust. This can be accomplished by either changing the actual certificate or by noting the title change in a minute entry, ledger, operating agreement, or business agreement.

Generally, the trust should be the beneficiary of all **insurance policies** if the death proceeds are to be distributed in accordance with the terms and conditions of the trust instrument. If the insurance policy is not beneficiaried correctly to the trust, or if no beneficiary designation is made, it is likely that the death proceeds will be transferred through probate. The owner of the insurance policy may or may not be an individual or a trustee, depending on whether the value of the policy and death proceeds are to be included in or excluded from the settlor's taxable estate.

Annuities, like insurance policies, should generally be beneficiaried to a trust if they are intended to be distributed under the terms and conditions of the trust instrument. The owner of the annuities should be the individual rather than a trust in order to circumvent any appearance of a taxable transfer. Although a grantor trust for tax purposes may hold an annuity, it is often less confusing to keep the settlor as the individual owner and simply change the beneficiary designation to the trust.

Tangible personal property does not generally have a title that can be changed, but the law allows it to be assigned, deeded, or transferred at death to a trust. Some tangible personal property may have certifications that may be formally transferred, such as specific pieces of artwork or musical instruments.

Automobiles must be retitled through the state (at your local license office) in the name of the trust or TOD to the trust in order for the trustee to take control of the vehicle. A trustee cannot endorse the title to an automobile in order to transfer the title unless the title is first in the name of the trust. This is true for boat titles, trailer titles, motorcycles, and any other vehicle with a title. Tractors and other equipment, however, do not have titles and must be assigned or transferred as tangible personal property.

Retirement accounts, although designated as custodial or trust accounts, cannot be titled in the name of a revocable living trust without triggering a taxable event. Accordingly, retirement accounts like IRAs, 401(k)s, 403(b)s, pensions, and profit sharing and benefit accounts must be held in individual names. Depending upon who the beneficiaries of the accounts are intended to be, a trust may or may not be the designated beneficiary. A trust may be the designated beneficiary upon the death of the individual or plan participant, but this should be done after carefully considering all of the tax and practical implications.

In order for an estate plan to function as intended, it is vitally important that all assets be titled and/or beneficiaried properly. Whenever a new asset is purchased, established, or created, the titling of the assets, as well as the beneficiary, must be inspected in order to verify that the asset will flow through the estate plan as intended. In the event that an individual is unable to complete the retitling of an asset, the person designated under a durable power of attorney may assist in the retitling in fulfilling his or her fiduciary duty in completing the estate plan.

Additionally, certain assets may need to be distributed directly to a spouse for tax purposes while other assets need to be held in trust for practical purposes. Therefore, the detailed review of how all assets are held, transferred, and beneficiaried is fundamental to a properly structured estate plan.

TRUST ADMINISTRATION

Q & A

Question 1: Who **administers a trust** after the settlor's death?
Answer: The successor trustee named in the document will administer the trust after he or she has accepted the duty.

Question 2: What **duties** must the successor trustee perform?
Answer: The successor trustee must manage the trust estate. This will require the trustee to make an inventory, pay taxes, pay debts, and distribute the income and principal based upon the terms and conditions set forth under the trust instrument.

During the settlor's lifetime, there is little to do regarding the administration of a revocable trust, since the settlor has full authority to revoke the trust, remove assets from the trust, and amend the trust in any way. As long as all of the assets are owned by the trust, the settlor may administer those assets through the trust at his or her full discretion.

Upon the **settlor's incapacity**, the successor trustee named under the instrument will take over the administration of the trust; when this occurs, the successor trustee must administer the trust under the terms and conditions set forth in the instrument. Typically, the successor trustee must use all of the trust assets for the benefit of the settlor's health, maintenance, and support in order to maintain the settlor within his or her accustomed standard of living. If any other persons are dependent upon the settlor, the trust instrument may authorize the trustee to also make distributions for their benefit.

Upon the **settlor's death**, the successor trustee will need to take all of the necessary steps to ensure that the settlor's affairs are put in order and that the trust is administered for the benefit of the beneficiaries named under the instrument. As a practical point, the first duty of the trustee will be to inform the family of the trustee's position and make arrangements for the **funeral** if no else has done so. An attorney should be contacted in order to assist in the trust administration and to advise the trustee of his or her duties and obligations to the beneficiaries.

In compliance with the Missouri Uniform Trust Code, the trustee has an obligation to **notify each beneficiary** of his or her respective rights to receive a copy of the trust instrument and a right to a periodic trust accounting. This notice must be tendered within 180 days of the settlor's death. The beneficiaries who are entitled to a current distribution of income or principal, i.e., permitted distributees, and those beneficiaries who would receive distributions if the current beneficiary's interests ended, i.e., qualified beneficiaries, must be ascertained and notified.

The trustee should begin his or her duties by creating a list of all of the settlor's debts and expenses that are outstanding. In the event that the trustee has knowledge of outstanding **debts, claims, or obligations**, the trustee must notify the creditors and make arrangements to review the debts and pay them if they are valid. All obligations, including existing or potential lawsuits, must be examined, and determination must be made as to whether legal counsel should be retained and what action should be taken regarding those obligations. If the trustee determines that a lawsuit must be addressed, he or she must notify the beneficiaries of the determination and explain its effect on the trust administration.

As a practical matter, the trustee should make arrangements to obtain several death certificates. This will be necessary in order to obtain payments, release assets of which the trust is the beneficiary, and transfer funds. If the trustee has not already been appointed, an appointment and **acceptance of trusteeship** should be signed by the successor trustee. This acceptance of trusteeship should be given to all financial institutions in order to establish the vesting of legal title in the name of the trustee. Once the successor trusteeship has been legally established, the trustee may begin negotiating trust bank accounts, brokerage accounts, real estate, business interests, and taking charge of tangible personal property. All backup trustees should be informed of their potential duty and be ready to assist in the trust administration if necessary.

If the settlor had any banked **genetic material**, the trustee should ascertain what the legal implications are regarding the material and if any jurisdiction will grant rights to potential heirs that may be born long after the settlor's death. These rights vary greatly in different jurisdictions. Currently, Missouri does not grant rights to persons who may be born after the normal time for gestation.

If the funeral home has not done so, the trustee should notify the United States Social Security Administration of the settlor's death and make arrangements to halt any future payments from the federal government. As a practical point of caution, the trustee should notify the major **credit reporting agencies** to prevent any theft of the decedent's identity. The trustee should also run a search on the unclaimed property website in each state where the decedent has lived to determine whether or not the decedent had any unclaimed property.

All **insurance** on the life of the settlor should be reviewed, and a claim for death benefits should be made. All **retirement accounts** must be reviewed, and the trustee should understand and assist in the distribution of the funds to the named beneficiaries. The retirement plan beneficiaries may affect the decedent's income and estate tax return, and, accordingly, the trustee must review all of the plan beneficiaries and distributions. Specifically, if any of the retirement plan beneficiaries are charities, the trustee must review the timing of the distributions with the chosen certified public accountant (CPA) or attorney.

If the settlor had rights, interests, or **benefits in any other trust** estates (such as a trust from a spouse or parent), the trustee must ascertain what benefits are vested in the estate of the decedent and analyze the tax and transfer consequences of those rights, if any. If the decedent is the recipient of trust income or principal from another trust, the trustee must determine who the successors are to those interests and should coordinate with the trustee of that trust.

Although **tangible personal property** rarely constitutes the greatest value in an estate, the transfer of tangible items such as jewelry, paintings, furniture, and other personal effects often has the highest emotional attachment. Because of the emotional attachment toward personal effects, the trustee must be careful to complete these transfers in a manner that will, if at all possible, mitigate any hard feelings among the beneficiaries. Most estate plans will have provided a method of transferring tangible personal property. This is usually done by a **signed list** describing the item along with the designation of the recipient and/or contingent recipient. Items not mentioned on the list are typically divided among the beneficiaries as they agree. In the event that there is a dispute regarding the distribution of the tangible personal property which cannot be resolved among the beneficiaries, the probate court can always be summoned to make a final determination of the same.

In order to properly allocate all of the debts, liabilities, taxes, income, and gains to the estate, the trustee must establish a **ledger** of accounts payable and income received. All of the trust assets must be **inventoried**. In addition, the assets must be valued or appraised, if necessary, for transfer and tax purposes. With regard to **real estate**, the property must be secured by maintaining insurance and kept safe from destruction or vandalism. The trustee should make sure that the keys to all structures are obtained and that the utilities are maintained as a matter of general upkeep. With regard to any **automobiles**, they should be secured until the titles to them are transferred. All automobiles should be insured while the trustee has custody over them. Caution would dictate that automobiles not be driven during the period that the title to them is being transferred.

In addition to the attorney being contacted, the settlor's **CPA** should be employed in order to review gift tax returns and prepare final income tax returns, fiduciary tax returns, a federal estate tax return, and a state inheritance tax return, if applicable. The CPA may be able to help with establishing valuations of various pieces of property. The trustee must report all income earned during the administration of the estate under a **1041** fiduciary tax return. This tax return will report income earned and show deductible distributions made to beneficiaries. This will require the tax preparer to obtain a separate **tax identification number** for the trust, if one has not previously been obtained. After the decedent's death, his or her social security number can no longer be used to report the estate's income.

In the event that the total value of the estate (including the trust, joint property, insurance benefits, retirement benefits, etc.) exceeds the applicable federal estate tax exemption (the basic exemption amount being $5 million in 2011), then the trustee must have a **706 federal estate tax return** prepared. The estate tax return is a detailed review of all of the assets included in the decedent's estate based upon his or her ownership interests in various properties, accounts, and interests. Precise valuations of all estate assets must be made as of the date of death, as well as the value of the assets six months after the date of death, i.e., the alternate valuation date (if taxes are due). This means that the trustee must have all of the assets appraised or valued by professionals in a manner that satisfies the IRS's criteria. Like any other tax return, certain transfers will qualify for deductions to the estate, and certain credits are granted to offset the ultimate tax due. For estate transfer purposes, the applicable credit, marital deduction, and generation-skipping tax exemption are the primary factors that affect the estate tax return. Any tax due must be paid within nine months of the decedent's death with the filing of the return or with an application for a six-month extension to file the entire return. If the estate contains assets that are of questionable value, transfers of questionable nature, or transactions that did not conform to IRS procedures, the estate may be audited in order to clarify the same. The audit period usually lasts for a three-year period after the return, if it is filed absent any fraud on behalf of the decedent or the estate.

Currently, the state of Missouri does not have a separate **state inheritance tax**. Formerly, the IRC granted a credit for state death taxes, which established the Missouri inheritance tax. Nevertheless, many states have retained separate inheritance taxes that are applicable to any properties located in or connected with their particular jurisdictions. The trustee must be aware of all potential tax liabilities and coordinate the filing of returns and the payment of taxes with the chosen tax preparer.

As a matter of local law, the trustee should have the attorney **file the settlor's will** with the probate court in the county of the decedent's residence. Depending upon creditor considerations and the necessity of transferring titles to various non-trusted assets, the trustee may decide to technically open a probate estate. This will necessitate the payment of various fees to the court and may require the personal representative under the will to be officially appointed by the court. Upon the **appointment of the personal representative**, he or she will have the legal authority to take charge of and transfer assets that were not previously titled in the name of the trust. In the event that the estate has not provided for the spouse or family, it may be possible to obtain a court order to make such a provision. Additionally, if the settlor failed to title an asset in the trust that is located in another state, the personal representative may open a probate administration in that other state, i.e., **ancillary administration**, and eventually transfer the title to that asset into the trust through a pour-over will.

When reviewing the estate administration with the beneficiaries of the estate, the trustee or his or her legal counsel should inform the beneficiaries of their respective rights to accept estate transfers, to disclaim estate assets, or to waive certain powers and interests. If any beneficiary deems the acceptance of estate assets to be unnecessary or unprofitable, that beneficiary may **renounce, waive, or disclaim** his or her interests or rights. Generally, this should be done early in the trust administration. If a designated person wishes to waive his or her right to serve in a certain capacity, this should be done before any confusion arises as to who the proper person is to negotiate trust affairs or assets. The beneficiary should be made aware of all time-sensitive waivers, renunciations, or disclaimers. Generally, federal and state laws require a person to sign a written disclaimer of assets within nine months of the decedent's death or nine months after a trust or interest becomes irrevocable. Additionally, the recipient of a right, asset, or interest must not accept the same and later try to disclaim it.

During the trust administration, and if sanctioned under the trust instrument, the trustee may take a **reasonable fee**, which is typically one percent of the trust value each year, or as determined under a corporate trustee fee schedule. This fee may vary or be delineated under the trust instrument. In the event that there is more than one trustee serving, the fee will usually be split among the trustees, unless the trust has designated otherwise or the beneficiaries agree otherwise. This fee will be deemed taxable income to the trustee, and, therefore, consideration must be given to the benefit of receiving income rather than principal if the trustee is also a beneficiary.

The trustee must remember that when he or she accepted the trusteeship of the trust estate, that trustee agreed to carry out the function as a **fiduciary** of the estate, which requires him or her to act in a manner that imposes a higher standard than is imposed upon himself or herself. This means that the trustee must refrain from all actions of self-dealing. The trustee must exercise care, as a prudent person would, in light of a duty of loyalty to the beneficiaries of the trust. All the terms and conditions contained within the trust instrument must be carried out in an efficient and reasonable manner. The trustee may not commingle his or her personal assets with the assets of the trust. The trustee must make sure that the trust assets are kept safe, made productive, and used wisely. The trustee must also invest and manage the trust assets in accordance with the Missouri Prudent Investor's Act.

After all taxes have been paid and a closing letter has been received from the IRS, state department of treasury, or local taxing agencies, the trustee can begin to **wind up the estate administration**. The trustee must also be sure that all creditor and claim periods against the trust have expired before the estate can be closed. All disputes among beneficiaries must be resolved and assets marshaled into the estate before the trustee can begin final distributions. This does not mean that the trustee cannot make partial distributions during the administration process when sufficient assets are retained to pay all trust obligations that are reasonably anticipated.

Prior to making any trust distributions, the trustee must render an accounting and **trust settlement** to the beneficiaries in order to inform them of the status of the administration in a manner that can be easily and precisely understood. In order to verify the beneficiary's receipt of a specific distribution, a written receipt should be signed by the beneficiary and filed with the trustee. When the beneficiaries have all received their respective distributions, signed receipts, and reviewed the trust settlement without objection, the trust administration can be terminated. If the trust instrument established secondary trusts for the benefit of a spouse, children, grandchildren, other persons, or charities, these subsequent trusts must have separate administrations that follow the general requirements of the initial trust administration.

Top 10 Planning Tips

1. A **health care directive** must be executed in order to give an agent the authority to make medical decisions, release medical information, and to withdraw or remove medical treatment.
2. An **agent, attorney-in-fact and trustee** must be honest, have common sense, and be able to organize the finances of the principal/settlor.
3. Trustees must keep an **accounting** of all trust affairs and should seek the assistance of competent tax, legal and investment counsel.
4. Corporations, limited partnerships, and limited liability companies generally will prevent the owner's assets from being attached by the entity's **creditors**.
5. The **rights and responsibilities** of shareholders, members, and partners should be set forth in a restrictive

stock agreement, operating agreement, or partnership agreement.

6. **Tax elections** for business and investment entities must be carefully analyzed with tax counsel or a CPA.

7. Most of a person's **assets should be retitled** or beneficiaried into a living trust.

8. Qualified assets and **retirement accounts** must be carefully reviewed in order to determine the appropriate primary and contingent beneficiaries.

9. Upon a settlor's incapacity, resignation, or death, the **successor trustee** must accept trusteeship and begin to administer the trust estate as dictated by the trust agreement. Legal and tax counsel should be retained by the successor trustee.

10. All **debts, taxes, and expenses** must be paid before any distributions are made to other beneficiaries. If trusts are to be established under the trust instrument, the trustee must establish the trust accounts and prepare for the taxation of those trusts.

CHAPTER THREE – ESTATE TRANSFERS IN GENERAL

In order to carry out the settlor's intention to minimize taxes and transfer costs, a properly planned estate should take advantage of the probate process, the non-probate transfer process, transfers in trust, and joint ownership transfers, if applicable.

THE PROBATE PROCESS

Q & A

Question 1: Does a will need to be **probated**?
Answer: Yes. If a decedent dies with assets in his or her sole name and has a valid will, the will should be probated by the probate court in the county of the decedent's residence. The probate court is the state agency that is granted the authority to oversee the administration of a will.

Question 2: What is the **probate process**?
Answer: The court will appoint a personal representative, require an inventory, require creditors to be notified, require heirs to be notified, oversee the disposition of the estate, and require a settlement or statement of account.

As previously described, the probate process oversees the disposition of property in the decedent's sole name with no designation for a transfer at death, such as joint ownership with right of survivorship. The probate process also applies to the management of assets for the benefit of a living individual who lacks capacity (due to age or disability) who has not appointed an agent or attorney-in-fact to transact business on his or her behalf. Finally, the probate process will apply to any transfer of assets at the death of an individual who did not use a trust or non-probate transfer to accomplish the transfer.

The probate process has the great benefit of ensuring that all transactions will be made under the **oversight of the court** and its administrative personnel. Every asset must be inventoried and each transfer reported to the court. The final distributions must be audited or approved by the court. Because of the protection and oversight of the estate administration, there are instances when the court's help may be sought.

For example, when family turmoil exists between the beneficiaries, it may be to everyone's benefit that the **court to review** and sanction all of the transactions and transfers from the estate. Only a court can make the final determination that a transaction has been properly accomplished within a statute of limitations time period. If a representative wishes to ensure that his or her actions will not result in any liability on that person's part, the probate court's determination will be binding on all parties and subject to appeals.

The probate court will ensure that all documents have been properly drafted and submitted and that appropriate orders are issued regarding them. The court will also ensure that the estate assets are distributed in **accordance with the last will** and testament. Additionally, the court will ensure that any settlement submitted is audited and has been made with mathematical correctness.

Because the probate process is exacting, the process itself takes a significant amount of time and can be costly to the estate if the personal representative and attorney take the statutory fees allowed to them. Nevertheless, the process will ensure that the administration of an estate is accomplished properly and that the **fees** sanctioned by the law have been paid. It should be noted that the probate process has generally been criticized because of the time and expense involved; notwithstanding the same, if an estate is properly administered, shortcuts should not be made, and fees must be paid for services rendered by professionals.

In order to comply with local law, the decedent's **last will and testament should be filed** with the probate court regardless of a probate administration being opened. Because there is a one-year time limit to open a probate administration, prudence would dictate that, at the very least, the will be probated. If this is done, a probate estate can be opened in a timely manner if an asset is later found which cannot be transferred in any other manner.

If a random asset is found that is titled solely in the name of a decedent, that asset will most likely need to be transferred under the terms of the individual's will and by a probate court order. In this instance, if a pour-over will had been executed, the asset would be **transferred to the trust** established by the decedent. On the other hand, if the decedent's will contained specific terms and conditions of distribution, those terms would control the disposition. The value of the asset to be probated will determine the complexity of the probate process, as well as the time and expense involved.

A properly constructed estate plan will make use of a will and may proceed with the opening of a probate estate, depending on the facts and circumstances at the time of the settlor's death.

TRANSFER/PAY ON DEATH: TOD AND POD

Q & A

Question 1: What is the common use of **non-probate transfers**?
Answer: Automobiles should have a TOD designation in order to avoid probate. Checking accounts should have POD designation in order to avoid probate.

As previously discussed, the Non-Probate Transfer Act will allow an asset to be transferred at the death of one or more individuals and distributed directly to the designated beneficiary. Many types of assets are more easily distributed under the Non-Probate Transfer Act than through a trust. For example, an automobile can easily be transferred at death by designating a beneficiary on the title of the automobile. Typically, the departments of motor vehicles prefer to transfer **vehicles by a TOD designation.**

Simple **checking accounts** can also be easily transferred through a **POD designation** by naming beneficiaries on the account statement. In this event, upon the death of the account owner, the beneficiary can have the account transferred into his or her name upon the presentation of the account owner's death certificate. The law will allow a joint bank account to be transferred upon the death of the surviving account owner to one or more beneficiaries. The use of a POD designation should generally be used for accounts that have relatively small balances.

A properly constructed estate plan will make use of the Non-Probate Transfer Act and will transfer some of the assets via POD or TOD designations. The ease and simplicity of the POD and TOD transfers each have their places in a well-thought-out estate plan.

BENEFICIARY DESIGNATIONS – FINANCIAL ACCOUNTS, ANNUITIES, AND RETIREMENT ACCOUNTS

Q & A

Question 1: On **what assets** should beneficiary designations be made?
Answer: Generally, retirement accounts, insurance policies, and annuities must have precise beneficiary designations.

Question 2: **How** should a beneficiary designation be made?
Answer: A beneficiary designation must be made on the appropriate beneficiary form or customized form. The beneficiary designation should list both the primary and contingent beneficiary.

Question 3: How are **retirement accounts paid out** to beneficiaries?
Answer: The rules for retirement account payouts are set forth under Section 401(a)(9) of the IRC.

Question 4: Who can **roll over** a retirement account?
Answer: Only a spouse can roll over a retirement account and continue to hold the account without distribution until the date that his or her retirement begins.

Question 5: What is a **stretch IRA**?
Answer: When a retirement account names certain persons as beneficiaries, those persons may withdraw the assets, and the payment is stretched over their respective life expectancies pursuant to IRC Section 401(a)(9).

Prior to the Non-Probate Transfer Act, financial contracts, annuities, retirement accounts, and insurance products of all types allowed for the transfer of rights and the distribution of assets by means of direct beneficiary designations. Most people expect that insurance death benefits will be **paid to the person designated on the beneficiary form**. Likewise, most people understand that the person listed under their IRA or retirement accounts will receive those remaining balances when the account holder dies. Nevertheless, most people are not careful to review their beneficiary designations to ensure that they achieve their overall estate planning goals and are in harmony with their other directives.

When using a revocable trust to direct most of the estate assets, there is no standard answer as to whether the trust should be the recipient of the proceeds of an insurance policy, annuity, or retirement account. This determination must be made after analyzing the overall estate objectives and tax implications.

When reviewing the distribution of **financial contracts and annuities**, the settlor must determine who should receive these assets at his or her death. The settlor must also review the income tax results at the time that these assets are transferred, distributed, and liquidated. The financial contract itself may allow certain people to receive the asset of a tax-favored basis, i.e., one in which the tax will be paid over time, deducted, or minimized. The attorney and CPA should be consulted when deciding how to transfer such an account. Generally, an annuity will be taxed at the time of transfer and/or distribution. In this event, the principal investment escapes taxation as return of principal while the growth within the contract is taxed as income. Therefore, the owner of the contract must determine whether a spouse, a trust, or another person should receive the proceeds under the contract in order to accomplish his or her estate and tax goals.

Retirement accounts of all types must be carefully scrutinized because of the detailed rules regarding distributions and taxation. Generally, retirement accounts must be held in the name of the individual account owner or plan participant. If the account is transferred into the name of a trust or estate, the IRS will deem this to be a taxable event. Accordingly, a retirement account, whether it is an IRA, 401(k), 403(b), pension plan, or defined benefit plan, will be held in the owner's or participant's name with a designated beneficiary to receive the fund upon the owner's or participant's death. This should not be confused with the retirement fund itself being administered in the name of either a retirement trust or custodial account. Because retirement benefits do not receive a step up in basis and are often **taxed as income when distributed**, the distribution of benefits must be analyzed in great detail.

IRC Sec. **401(a)(9)** sets forth in great detail how certain retirement plans must be distributed. The IRC has established the rules for the taxation of retirement benefits when the owner withdraws the funds from the account or takes a distribution. Generally, the owner may transfer a set amount of income into a retirement account, and the account may grow and accumulate income while deferring taxes until a withdrawal is made.

Generally, an account owner may not withdraw funds from his or her retirement account until they reach **age 59 ½** without a ten percent penalty. There are exceptions to this rule, most notably the ability to make periodic annual withdrawals under IRC Sec. **72(t)**. Once the account owner reaches age 59 ½, he or she may withdraw funds without an early withdrawal penalty. The taxation of withdrawals is generally taxed at the owner's income tax rate, but exceptions are made for the withdrawal of qualified employer stock within the account; in this event, the distribution of stock may receive capital gains treatment.

After an owner has reached his or her **required beginning date**, that owner must begin withdrawals from his or her retirement account. This is generally April 1 following the owner reaching the age of 70 ½. Upon this occurrence, the owner must withdraw a minimum distribution based upon his or her life expectancy, and although the owner may take more out at any time, the entire distribution is subject to additional taxation at the owner's marginal tax rate.

If the account owner dies before he or she has withdrawn the balance from the account, IRC Sec. 401(a)(9) has detailed requirements for withdrawal and taxation of the funds, depending on who the designated beneficiary is and on whether the owner dies before or after the required beginning date. In order to ensure that an individual's retirement plan is properly integrated into his or her estate plan, the **beneficiary designation** of each IRA, 401(k), pension plan, or other retirement plan must be analyzed. This requires a review of who should receive the retirement fund, what the tax implications of the beneficiary designation are, and in what manner the proceeds may be distributed.

In most instances where a **husband and wife** have been married for long time and have common children, the spouse will be designated as the beneficiary under the owner's account. This general proposition may change depending upon family dynamics and personal aspirations. For example, someone who has been divorced and remarried with children from other marriages may not want his or her spouse to be the beneficiary of his or her entire retirement account.

The spouse, as the designated beneficiary, is the only person who may receive retirement benefits from his or her deceased spouse as a result of a direct **spousal rollover**. In this event, the spouse may have the retirement accounts transferred directly into his or her own account and thereby defer distributions until the required beginning date. Only a spouse or a qualified terminal interest property **(QTIP) trust** may obtain a spousal rollover. If a distribution to a QTIP trust is chosen, the beneficiary designation must be properly worded to direct the distribution to the trust, and the trust must be drafted in a manner that meets the requirements of both the marital deduction regulations and the required minimum distribution regulations (RMDs).

The federal rules under the Employee Retirement Income Security Act (ERISA) require that, if the participant is married, his or her spouse must be the designated beneficiary under the participant's employer's sponsored plans. This requirement may only be waived by the spouse pursuant to a written **spousal consent**. This rule, however, does not apply to IRAs. Nevertheless, if the spouse is listed as the designated beneficiary of the retirement benefit, the spouse will receive the benefit regardless of a subsequent divorce or the owner's contrary intentions.

The rules for the taxation of retirement withdrawals for beneficiaries are complex and must be reviewed by tax counsel. Generally, if a non-spouse is the beneficiary, there is no rollover with the deferral of taxation. The rules for **inherited retirement accounts** must be reviewed in detail, and beneficiary designation must be made in accordance with the owner's desires and tax plan. Under the Pension Protection Act of 2006, the rules for distributions from 401(k)s to IRAs and inherited IRAs was given greater flexibility; nevertheless, the rules must be reviewed periodically to ensure minimum taxation without penalty.

If children or other descendants are named beneficiaries, the retirement distribution may be **stretched out** over the life expectancy of the beneficiary. This will allow the beneficiary to voluntarily withdraw the account slowly and thereby pay income tax at a slow rate. This distribution schedule, however, is not required, and the beneficiary may withdraw the entire balance subject to taxation on the entire fund. If a beneficiary chooses to stretch out his or her distribution, that person will find that the account will grow on a tax-deferred basis, and the taxation will be minimized over a long period of time.

In the event that an account owner wishes for the **children to receive his or her retirement** benefits at that person's death or the subsequent death of that person's spouse, and the children are minors, special attention must be given to the account in order for it to not be placed into a conservatorship estate under the supervision of the probate court. In this event, a trust can be designated as the beneficiary of the account if the trust is drafted in compliance with the applicable IRC regulations.

In order for a **trust to qualify as a designated beneficiary**, the trust must adhere to the following rules: (1) the trust must be valid under state law, (2) the trust is irrevocable or will become irrevocable upon the death of the account owner or plan participant, (3) the beneficiaries of the trust are identifiable from the trust instrument with respect to the trust's interest in the retirement benefit, (4) the plan administrator is provided with the necessary documentation, and (5) all beneficiaries must be individuals by the beneficiary finalization date.

When beneficiaries of the trust and corresponding retirement account are minors, spendthrifts, or those simply unable to manage finances, a trust can be used as a **conduit** for the retirement distributions. In this event, the trust could distribute the greater of the income or the minimum required distribution to the beneficiary. The trustee, however, would control the distribution of amounts over the income or required minimum distributions (RMDs), perhaps based upon a power to encroach upon the corpus of the fund for the beneficiary's health, education, maintenance, and support.

If the trust beneficiary has met the requirements of the trust terms, it may be possible for the trustee to **renounce** the retirement plan distribution in favor of the account or plan proceeds to be distributed directly to the beneficiary. In any event, if the beneficiary does not wish to receive the retirement account, he or she may **disclaim** his or her respective interests, and the proceeds will be distributed to the contingent beneficiary.

In the event that the owner or plan participant wished to distribute the account to a beneficiary at his or her death as a conduit trust with specific powers of encroachment, an individual **retirement plan trust** may be created and designated as the beneficiary of the retirement plan. This type of trust meets all of the criteria set forth under the IRC and corresponding regulations and must be correctly linked to the plan or account via a properly worded beneficiary form.

In the event that a retirement account has no designated beneficiary or the beneficiary is the "estate," the proceeds will be distributed through the owner's or participant's **probate estate**. In this event, the estate does not qualify as an individual and may not be rolled over or stretched out over the beneficiary's lifetime. Most likely, the proceeds will have to be distributed under the **five-year rule** set forth in the IRC.

The applicable regulations allow the **beneficiaries of a retirement plan to be designated** by September 30 after the year of the account owner's or participant's death, and the **separate shares must be established** by December 31 of that same year. Because the regulations allow this time for the designation and establishment of separate shares, it is possible for a non-individual, e.g., a charity receiving a percentage of the benefits, to receive its distribution by the required date and thereby allow the remaining individual beneficiaries to stretch out their respective distributions. Based upon these rules, a charity may be listed as a designated beneficiary for all or a portion of the retirement proceeds. In the event that a person wants to make **charitable gifts** at his or her death, the distribution of a retirement benefit is a very tax-efficient method of doing so. In this event, a qualifying charity who receives the retirement benefit will not pay an estate tax or any income tax.

Roth IRAs hold a special advantage, since they are distributed free of taxation (having previously been taxed). Accordingly, Roth IRAs may be distributed through trust more easily than traditional IRAs without as much tax analysis. Nevertheless, the rules applicable to Roth IRAs must also be reviewed with tax counsel for all of the same reasons as any other retirement account.

An effective estate plan must carefully review all retirement benefits, annuities, insurance policies, and other contracts, noting who the desired beneficiaries are and by what means the benefits should be transferred to them. If these types of assets are not integrated into the estate plan, they could pass to the incorrect beneficiary, pass through probate, or be taxed in a manner less favorable than the owner contemplated.

REVOCABLE LIVING TRUSTS

Q & A

Question 1: Does a person lose **control of his or her assets** if they are titled in a revocable living trust?
Answer: No. The settlor retains full control over the use and disposition of the trust assets during his or her lifetime and competency.

Question 2: Does a revocable living trust need to be **probated**?
Answer: Generally, no; the trust law provides for a trust to be administered and distributed without the necessity of court approval. The probate court does retain jurisdiction in order to intervene if necessary.

Question 3: Does a revocable living trust provide **creditor protection**?
Answer: Generally, no; if the settlor can gain access to the trust assets, so can his or her respective creditors. However, once the trust becomes irrevocable and is held for the benefit of someone other than the settlor, a sub-trust may be established as a discretionary trust or as a spendthrift trust that may provide protection of the assets from the creditors of the beneficiary.

Question 4: Does a revocable living trust provide for **tax planning**?
Answer: The taxation of a trust depends on how the trust is structured. Depending on whether the trust is a "grantor trust" for tax purposes is important. The use of tax laws within the trust depends on the drafting of the trust instrument.

Question 5: What **provisions** can be made for children, descendants, and other beneficiaries under a trust agreement?
Answer: A trust agreement is very flexible; almost anything that is not against public policy may be drafted into a trust agreement.

Question 6: How is a revocable living trust **revoked or modified**?
Answer: The terms of the trust instrument will dictate how the trust may be modified. Generally, the settlor may revoke a trust as long as he or she remains competent.

The use of a revocable living trust as the primary vehicle for managing and distributing an individual's estate has greatly increased over the last 25 years. Most people with an estate over $250,000 should review the use of a trust in order to (1) avoid probate; (2) ensure that a trustee is named who can pay debts, taxes, and expenses at the settlor's death; and (3) establish separate shares with contingent plans directed in detail.

Revocable trusts provide an **easy method of managing assets** that have been titled in the trust and allow great flexibility in control and withdrawal. The settlor may revoke the trust, withdraw assets at any time, and amend the provisions of the instrument for as long as he or she is competent.

In the event that an individual desires to hold assets for the benefit of a spouse, child, or loved one, a trust is a great vehicle to do so. Generally, the terms and conditions of a trust are **not subject to public scrutiny**, and the probate court does not need to get involved unless there has been a breach of trust. A trust can easily establish sub-trusts upon the death of the settlor based upon tax laws, family planning, or simply the general intent of the settlor.

A well-drafted trust will always provide for the payment of the settlor's debts, taxes, and expenses. Generally, all of the enforceable **debts** of the settlor will be paid by the trustee. Debts may include utilities, bills, notes, and other obligations. If the trust instrument specifically dictates, debts may include the payment of mortgages.

Expenses of the settlor may include the costs of a funeral and ceremony, as well as fees incurred by the trust in the administration of an estate. Trustee fees, attorney fees, accounting fees, and financial advisor fees will typically be paid from the trust assets. Certain management and transmission fees will be paid from the trust and receive deductions on the trust 1041 tax return.

The trust should be directed to pay all **taxes** associated with the estate administration and distribution, as well as any taxes owed by the settlor prior to his or her death. Accordingly, the trustee should oversee the preparation of the settlor's last 1040 tax return. If any income tax, capital gains tax, penalties, or interest is due, the trustee must ensure that they are properly paid.

The trustee will be granted the authority to sign the decedent's tax return. In particular, the trust should grant the trustee the authority to allocate the decedent's tax credits and take any deductions available to the estate. For estate tax purposes, the trustee must be given the authority to prepare and file a **706 federal estate tax return** and any corresponding **state inheritance tax return**. With regard to these returns, the trustee will need to seek the counsel of a tax advisor familiar with federal and state estate taxes.

If the settlor was a US citizen, the trustee should allocate the **basic exclusion amount** toward the distributions to those beneficiaries receiving distributions within that threshold. Under the 2010 Tax Relief Act, the basic exclusion is $5 million (along with any unused exclusion of a spouse which may be ported over to the surviving spouse, i.e., the applicable exclusion). This means that a person may transfer up to $5 million during life or at death without any transfer tax being imposed. Most trusts will take advantage of this tax credit and direct that the exclusion amount be held in a trust for the benefit of a spouse, children, or other loved ones. This type of trust is commonly referred to as a **residuary trust**, family trust, B trust, or credit shelter trust.

If the settlor was married and the spouse is a US citizen, the estate may allocate an unlimited **marital deduction** amount toward a qualifying distribution. Under the 2011 Tax Act, the marital deduction is **unlimited** and is granted if the distribution is made outright or held in trust, meeting the requirement contained under IRC Section 2056(b)(7). This means that a person may transfer any amount to a spouse without gift or estate tax. Most trust will take advantage of this tax deduction and direct that the deductible amount be held in a trust for the benefit of the spouse, granting him or her the right to require that **all income** be distributed to him or her and for encroachment of principal for health, maintenance, and support. This type of trust is commonly referred to as a **marital deduction trust** or qualified terminal interest property **(QTIP) trust**.

If the settlor's spouse is not a US citizen, the federal law requires that the surviving spouse's inheritance be held in a special type of trust known as a **Qualified Domestic Trust (QDT)**. Under this type of trust, the assets (1) must be held in trust by at least one US citizen or trust company, (2) require the payment of estate taxes at the death of the spouse, (3) allow the trustee to withhold tax on any distribution to the spouse, (4) require the trustee to comply with all the regulations for a marital deduction trust, and (5) require that an election be made by the trustee/executor to meet the requirements of IRC Section 2056 (A).

The use of both the marital deduction and the basic exclusion amount is standard operating procedure under most estate plans. By taking advantage of these laws, there should be no tax at the death of the first spouse, and there is assurance that up to $5 million may be sheltered from estate taxes in each spouse's estate. This is commonly referred to as **A/B tax planning** within a trust or estate plan.

In the event that the settlor desires to transfer assets to his or her grandchildren or other persons 37 ½ years younger than he or she, that person will have to consider the ramifications of the **Generation-Skipping Transfer Tax**. Under IRC Chapter 13 Sec. 2601-2664, the rules for generation-skipping transfers are set forth. Generally, Congress has tried to circumvent transfers of estate assets to younger or skipped generations, since these persons will not pay transfer taxes for many years to come. Accordingly, transfers that skip a generation, e.g., transfers to grandchildren, are subject to another tax in addition to the estate tax (if they exceed the GST exemption amount). This tax is at the same rate as the estate tax. These transfers may be outright or in trust. The transfer may be a direct skip or an indirect skip. For example, a direct transfer to a grandchild is a direct skip, while a transfer in trust that grants a child the right to income and principal for life and distributes (taxable distributions) or terminates (taxable terminations) in favor of a grandchild is an indirect skip. All of these transfers are subject to the GST tax. Fortunately, the 2010 Tax Relief Act has increased the **GST exemption** to $5 million. This means that a person may transfer up to $5 million, either outright or in trust, to "skip persons", as defined by the IRC. In the event that a person wishes to leave more than the GST exemption amount to grandchildren, for example, then the trust would typically contain language creating both GST-exempt sub-trusts (which would not be subject to the GST tax) and GST non-exempt sub-trusts (which would be subject to the GST tax). For example, a typical GST-exempt sub-trust would grant a child the right to all of the income and principal for health, education, maintenance, and support for his or her lifetime, after which the child's descendant(s) would be granted the same or a similar right. Because the MUTC allows trusts to continue into perpetuity, a GST trust may have no end.

In the event that a married couple's estate is less than the basic exemption amount, a **joint revocable trust** can be used to avoid probate, manage the estate, and distribute the assets to children under customized terms and conditions. Under this type of trust, the settlors would each retain full control over the trust until both of them had died. A joint trust established between a husband and wife will receive the benefit of creditor protection afforded tenants by the entireties. Each settlor could revoke the trust, withdraw assets, and amend the trust. The survivor's basic exemption amount would cover any transfer taxes attributable to the estate. It is theoretically possible for a portion of the joint trust assets or the assets contributed by a particular settlor to be segregated at the first spouse's death to fund A/B tax planning; this may be accomplished by using a **Qualified Spousal Trust.**

Whether a joint trust or separate trusts are used after the surviving spouse's subsequent death, the estate will typically be transferred to children, loved ones, or charities. For example, it is common planning for an estate to be segregated into **separate trusts for the benefit of each of the settlor's children.** This amount may be equal or in varying percentages or fractions.

Typically, the trustee is granted the authority to distribute income and principal for the beneficiary's health, education, maintenance, and support. Distributions for **health** would include payment for dentists, doctors, and other health care needs. **Educational spending** is typically very broad and includes primary, secondary, and post-graduate schooling. The **maintenance** of the beneficiary, with regard to housing and essential food and clothing, is granted. Additionally, the **support** of the beneficiary in a lifestyle to which he or she is accustomed is authorized, including appropriate transportation and necessities.

Many times, the **principal distributions** of a child's trust are not made until the child has reached an age that the settlor deems appropriate, e.g., one-third at age 25, one-half at age 30, and the balance upon reaching the age of 35. The formula for trust distributions is very flexible and may, for example, contain provisions as restrictive as (1) requiring drug testing before distributions are made, (2) requiring the beneficiary to earn a certain wage, (3) requiring the beneficiary to complete a certain level of education, or (4) requiring the beneficiary to demonstrate the ability to use wealth in a responsible manner. All restrictions are subject to public policy standards but may be very creative in nature as long as the trustee is able to reasonably carry them out. The trust may authorize the trustee to be very generous in the distribution of principal, e.g., granting the trustee authority to make distributions to children (1) to start a business, (2) to get married, or (3) to purchase a home.

Distributions from the trust may include **specific pecuniary** (dollar) amounts to be made outright or held in trust for any individual the settlor wishes. For example, the trust may provide that $250,

000 be held in trust for the settlor's nephew for his education. In this instance, the settlor's available basic exemption amount could circumvent any estate tax on such a bequest.

A trust may also provide for a **charitable bequest** to be made which, if made properly, should not result in any estate tax. All bequests to qualifying 501(c) charities ascertainable from the terms of the trust should qualify for the charitable estate tax deduction. A charitable distribution may be simple or complex, depending upon the settlor's intention and the tax savings to be achieved. For example, a simple bequest of $50,000 to the Red Cross would qualify as a charitable deduction and would reduce the estate for tax purposes. Likewise, a charitable remainder trust or charitable lead trust could be constructed within the primary trust instrument to be established only after the settlor's death. These types of trusts could qualify for a partial charitable deduction depending upon their terms and conditions dictated by the trust provisions, i.e., length of term.

In the event that a settlor wishes to **distribute his or her retirement plan through trust** to a spouse, a QTIP trust could be the recipient. This may be done if the settlor does not wish for his or her spouse to receive the retirement account outright. The **QTIP trust** will require all of the income, i.e., all of the minimum distributions, to be distributed over the lifetime of the spouse, which may result in the spouse receiving the balance of the retirement account anyway. In the event that the settlor wishes to distribute his or her retirement plan through trust for the benefit of his or her children, that person may do so by complying with the 401(a)(9) regulations. Separate shares may be established for children, but each child will be required to take his or her distribution over the lifetime of the oldest child. These types of retirement trust distributions are typically structured as a **conduit** that distributes the greater of the RMD or the trust income.

Regardless of the type of sub-trust created for a spouse, child, or entity, the trust should apply the **spendthrift** law to the trust share in order to ensure that the beneficiary's creditors cannot reach the trust assets. This law provides that the beneficiary's creditors may not reach either a voluntary or involuntary transfer of the beneficiary's interest. A creditor must therefore wait for the trust to make a distribution to the beneficiary before that amount may be attached.

A judgment for spousal or child support may only attach the trust's income.

The trust will provide a method of determining if the settlor is **incapacitated** and who the successor trustee is in that event. Typically, the trust will provide that a physician will need to determine incapacity, and that determination must be reduced to a written statement.

Upon the settlor resigning, becoming incapacitated, or dying, the named successor may accept trusteeship and begin the duties outlined in the trust instrument. The **successor trustee** may be one or more individuals, a corporate trustee, or a combination of the two. The duties of the trustee should be designated in the trust instrument, and provision for trustee resignation and delegation of duties should be delineated. The designation of who should administer the trust if a settlor is no longer able to act or has died should be carefully considered. The workability of the trustees should be analyzed to make sure the trust will be administered with ease and without internal conflict.

The settlor, as well as all successor trustees, will be granted the **trust powers** and authorities contained in the trust instrument. Although the MUTC grants broad powers, the trust instrument itself should delineate the trustee powers in detail in order for financial institutions to clearly see each power that may be required.

When structuring an estate plan between a husband and wife, the plan will typically be triggered by the death of one spouse. Therefore, in the event of a simultaneous death, the law allows the trust instrument to designate which spouse predeceased the other. This is known as a **simultaneous death** clause. The order of death should be reviewed in order to accomplish the spouse's plan in light of taxes, as well as the actual distributions that will take place at the second death.

The trust instrument must designate who is able to **revoke** the trust, who may **withdraw** assets, and who may **amend and modify** the trust instrument. In some instances, the trust may allow a settlor's attorney-in-fact, under his or her durable power of attorney, the ability to revoke, withdraw, and amend the document within the attorney-in-fact's fiduciary duty toward the settlor. While the settlor retains the ability to revoke his or her trust, that person has full control and dominion over the trust and the trust assets. The settlor may do anything he or she wishes with the trust and the trust property without restriction.

Because of the flexibility of a revocable living trust, this type of instrument has become the estate planning document most commonly used. In consideration of the privacy granted a trust, the avoidance of probate, and the flexibility granted under the MUTC, most people with any sizeable estate will use a revocable living trust as the hub of their estate plans.

DISCLAIMERS
Q & A

Question 1: Is a beneficiary **required to accept a distribution** made to him or her?
Answer: No. A beneficiary may refuse to accept any distribution. If the beneficiary waives that right within the time limits and according to the processes set forth under state and federal law, the waiver will qualify as a disclaimer and be made to the contingent beneficiary.

Question 2: May a disclaimant **direct who will receive** the property he or she disclaimed?
Answer: No. The disclaimed property must be distributed to the next beneficiary in line to receive the property as if the disclaimant had predeceased him or her.

Once a person has died or a trust has become irrevocable, the beneficiaries of the interest have a certain time in which they may technically and legally **refuse to accept** their distributions, rights, or inheritances. This right of refusal is known as a disclaimer and is subject to statutory requirements and will only become effective if those requirements are met.

Pursuant to R.S.Mo. Sections 469.010-340, any individual who may receive an interest in property from another person may disclaim **all or a portion** of the transfer. Unless the terms of the transfer indicate otherwise, the transfer of disclaimed property shall cause the property to be distributed **as if the disclaimant had died immediately before** the transfer. Accordingly, the transfer is deemed to have passed directly from the transferor to the ultimate takers.

A disclaimer is made in writing showing an unconditional refusal to accept a transfer and must be **signed** by the disclaimant or the disclaimant's representative. The written disclaimer must be delivered within **nine months** after the transfer and **before acceptance**. For this purpose, acceptance of a transferred interest or a portion of it may be shown by conduct, including acceptance of benefits. Acceptance precludes a disclaimer becoming effective. Acceptance may be made on behalf of a person by that person's representative, e.g., an attorney-in-fact, fiduciary, trustee, guardian, or conservator.

Each **separate interest** in property may be disclaimed or accepted, including specific amounts, parts, fractions, proportions, or amounts based upon formulas. **Contingent future interests** may also be disclaimed in whole or in part; this, however, must be accomplished within nine months after the beneficiary has been ascertained and his or her interest is vested. If an interest does not legally belong to a beneficiary, that beneficiary has no right to disclaim.

In the event that an interest is disclaimed, the interest will be distributed to **the next beneficiary in line** to receive the distribution either based upon a beneficiary designation or by law. If no beneficiary designation is found, the disclaimant's heirs may take the interest, which may require the opening of a probate estate. Generally, if an interest is vested in a person who has not reached the age of 21, the interest is subject to disclaimer until nine months after the person's 21st birthday.

The **IRC Sec. 2518** sets forth the same rules that the Missouri statutes contain regarding the law of disclaimers. The federal law recognizes that a person cannot be forced to accept a gift or inheritance. Therefore, a disclaimer, if it meets the requirements, is not treated as a gift or transfer. Like the Missouri requirement, the disclaimer must be irrevocable, unqualified, and in writing. The nine-month period is the same, and the disclaimant must not have accepted the transfer. The disclaimed property must be distributed to the correct party. The property must pass to someone **other than the disclaimant** as a result of the disclaimer. As an additional result of the disclaimer, the property must pass to the recipient **without any direction on the part of the disclaimant.**

Disclaimers are helpful in **diverting property interests** in many instances, such as when (1) the interest is not needed by the beneficiary, (2) the interest will result in an adverse tax consequence to the beneficiary, (3) the interest would be better utilized for tax purposes by the contingent beneficiary, or (4) diverting the property would fulfill the transferor's estate plan. When a property interest has not been properly designated, a disclaimer may be able to solve the problem.

Disclaimers should be used with caution and only after a **review of who the contingent beneficiaries** are. Since the disclaimant cannot direct the transfer, the legal flow of distribution must be analyzed. The nine-month **time limit** for disclaimers is strict and nonnegotiable. Although the formalities of a disclaimer are relatively easy, they must be adhered to as well. Generally, the beneficiary of an irrevocable trust must disclaim his or her interest within nine months of the trust becoming irrevocable, which means that the beneficiary of a revocable trust must disclaim within nine months of the settlor's death.

INSURANCE AND INSURANCE TRUSTS

Q & A

Question 1: When is insurance recommended for **estate planning**?
Answer: Having insurance of various types should depend upon the individual's stage in life. If a person has mortgages and debts, insurance may be used to provide security to loved ones. If liquidity is needed to fund certain business or personal plans, insurance may be used for that funding. If estate taxes are anticipated, insurance may be used to offset those taxes.

Question 2: Is insurance **taxable** in a person's estate?
Answer: The taxation of insurance depends upon the ownership of the insurance. If an individual retains incidents of ownership, the death proceeds will be included in that individual's taxable estate. The death proceeds may escape income taxation.

Question 3: Why should a person consider establishing an **irrevocable life insurance trust (ILIT)**?

Answer: An ILIT, if structured properly, will own the insurance within it and circumvent the inclusion of the death proceeds from the insured's taxable estate. An ILIT may also be structured to hold and distribute trust assets to beneficiaries in conformity with the insured's overall estate plan.

Question 4: Are premium payments made to an ILIT subject to **gift taxes**?
Answer: That depends upon how the ILIT was drafted. If the beneficiaries have a current right to withdraw the premium payments, that right should be considered a gift for annual gift tax exclusion purposes.

Life insurance plays a large part in estate planning, since the death benefits can have a substantial impact on the **cash needs** of the family and the tax consequences to the estate. The need for life insurance varies from individual to individual and changes as a person's estate increases. When a person first acquires an estate and family, life insurance is needed to **pay off liabilities** in case of death. For example, a young couple with children should have life insurance to provide extra funds in the event that one of them dies. In this example, the payment of mortgages, bills, and providing liquidity for future expenditures is important. For the business owner, the need for an influx of cash at the key person's death will be important to ensure that the **business will be tided over** until it can re-establish itself. For those who have a taxable estate at their death, insurance may provide a way to have the cash to **pay estate taxes**.

In order to evaluate an insurance policy, one must first ascertain who the **owner** of the policy is. The owner should be listed on the policy, have an insurable interest, and be able to control the policy. The owner may designate or change beneficiaries and may control the investment of the policy assets, if any. The **insured** under the policy must also be reviewed. The insured is the person against whose life the insurance is secured. When the insured dies, the policy is triggered and the death benefit paid. Finally, the **beneficiary** is the person or entity who will receive the death benefit upon the death of the insured.

For estate planning purposes, when reviewing life insurance, an analysis of who the owner of the policy is and who the primary and contingent beneficiaries are is crucial in evaluating taxation of that insurance. The IRC requires the value of the insurance death benefit to be included in the insured's taxable estate if the policy was either owned by the insured or the insured had any incidents of ownership. The incidents of ownership may include owning an insurance policy within a trust that is revocable, amendable, or may be directed by the insured.

Although many people understand that insurance proceeds are generally income tax free, a common misconception is that the death benefits are also tax free. To the contrary, if a person owns a life insurance contract, the death benefit will be included in that person's taxable estate. On the other hand, if a person, including the insured, does not own the life insurance contract on his or her life, then the death benefit will not be included in that person's taxable estate. The evaluation of whether the life insurance proceeds are included in one's estate is critical to any estate tax analysis.

Generally, life insurance death benefits can be excluded from an insured's estate by **purchasing a policy on a third party's life or transferring the policy to a third party**. For example, a person could purchase an insurance policy on the life of his or her parent, and the death benefit would not be included in that parent's taxable estate. This simple process may be effective but could result in several unforeseen problems. If a third party, such as a child, owns insurance on the life of a parent, the policy (1) may be transferred by the third party contrary to the insured's desire; (2) the cash value may be withdrawn by the third party; (3) the policy may lapse through neglect or disregard; or (4) the cash values may become subject to the third party's creditors, including a spouse in a divorce proceeding.

In many instances, the safest third party ownership is an irrevocable life insurance trust that requires the trustee to hold the policy under a fiduciary obligation toward the policy and the underlying beneficiaries. As long as the policy was purchased by the trustee as a third party, the death benefits will not be included in the insured's taxable estate. With regard to existing policies, the death benefits will likewise escape taxation after three years of transfer. Accordingly, if death occurs within three years of the transfer of an existing policy, the death benefit will be included in the taxable estate of the insured/owner regardless of the new owner being an individual or an irrevocable insurance trust.

An **irrevocable life insurance trust**, commonly referred to as an ILIT, has many benefits as the owner and beneficiary of an insurance contract. In order for the trust to direct the policy and the death benefit, the trustee must be the designated owner and beneficiary. Upon this occurrence, the trustee has a **fiduciary obligation to pay the premiums** for the policy and to maintain the policy so that it will not lapse. The **trustee** may be an individual, a corporate trustee, or an individual and corporate trustee acting together. The trustee should be given authority to collect the policy proceeds and may then invest the proceeds as is prudent.

The trust will dictate who will **ultimately receive the death benefits** as primary and contingent beneficiaries. Distributions from the ILIT can be made in the same way as any other trust, e.g., to children or grandchildren held in trust for their benefit. These decisions should be made carefully, however, since the trust is irrevocable. Once the disposition of the policy proceeds is set forth in the trust instrument, it cannot be changed, other than through an amendment by the beneficiaries under MUTC Section 456.4A-411 if the settlor is alive and consents or under MUTC Section 456.4B-411 by the beneficiaries with the court's approval.

If for some reason the policy proceeds are included in the insured's estate, the trustee may be given the authority to pay taxes in the insured's estate; otherwise, the policy proceeds will not be used to directly pay taxes. Typically, the policy proceeds may be used by the trustee to either **loan** to the insured estate to pay taxes or to **purchase assets** from the insured's estate in order to provide liquidity to pay taxes.

Because the policy was purchased by a third party, i.e., the trustee, the policy proceeds will **not be included** in the insured's/settlor's estate, no matter how large the death benefit. Likewise, as long as the policy was transferred more than three years before the insured's/settlor's death, the death benefit will not be included in the insured's/settlor's estate and escape taxation under the IRC.

The payment of policy premiums would normally be subject to **gift taxes** because the beneficiaries under the trust do not have a current right to receive any benefit under the trust; therefore, the insured's annual gift tax exclusion is inapplicable. A gift is only established if a person makes a current transfer, not a future transfer, giving up dominion and control of the interest transferred. Because the distribution of policy proceeds will not be made until after the insured's death, there is no current transfer of any interest; therefore, there is no gift toward which to apply the gift tax exclusion.

There is an exception to this gift tax rule that was established under a famous case entitled *Crummey v. Commissioner of Internal Revenue*. Under this case, the tax court ruled that a gift of the policy premium is in fact made to the beneficiaries if the beneficiaries are given a current right to receive the premium payment. This is commonly referred to as a **Crummey right of withdrawal**, named after the case. This right of withdrawal must be actually given and may impose a time limit upon the beneficiaries to take the premium before it is applied to the insurance policy. The tax court has also acquiesced to the power holders to include contingent beneficiaries. Therefore, the right to withdrawals pursuant to Crummey notices may, for example, include spouses, children, and grandchildren, thereby increasing the number of annual exclusions that may be used to offset larger premium payments.

As a practical matter, the trustee receives notice that the policy premiums are due. The trustee requests the payment of the premium from the insured and deposits the premium in a trust bank account under a separate tax ID number. In turn, the trustee notifies the beneficiaries, referred to as withdrawal right power holders, of their **right to withdraw the premium within a certain time limit**, for example 30 days. If the power holders do not request a distribution of the premium within the specified time limit, the trustee may proceed to **pay the insurance company the premium due.** Because the power holders had a current right to withdraw the premium, a current gift was established in favor of the power holder, and the insured may apply his or her annual gift tax exclusion ($14,000 per individual) against each power holder's right to withdraw. Hence, **no gift tax** will be accessed against the payment of the premium, and **no estate tax** will be assessed against the death benefit paid at the death of the insured.

In the event that a person calculates his or her estate to be large enough to incur an estate tax, that person could establish an ILIT and have the trustee purchase insurance that would roughly **cover his or**

her estate tax exposure. Upon the insured's death, the trustee could either lend cash to the estate or purchase assets from the estate in order to **provide liquidity** to pay estate taxes due nine months after the decedent's death. The assets remaining in the ILIT after the loan or purchase would be administered under the terms and conditions contained in the ILIT. If the Crummey notices have been properly sent and acknowledged, and the policy was purchased properly or transferred in a timely manner, there should be no gift or estate tax associated with the ILIT or the policy it holds.

It should be remembered that the ILIT will most likely administer assets received from the loans to the estate, purchased from the estate, or cash **invested for many years** to come if held in trust. Therefore, the terms of the trust and the investment powers of the trustee must be thorough and broad enough to take care of any future contingencies. The assets in an insurance trust may be used for any purpose set forth under the trust instrument, including continuing a business, supporting individual beneficiaries, or assisting the estate by providing cash.

It is common for the assets in an ILIT to be held for the **benefit of the insured's spouse** for his or her lifetime, giving that person rights to income and principal for health, education, maintenance, and support. These assets are generally free from predators and creditors and are not included in the spouse's taxable estate if his or her encroachment is limited to an ascertainable standard. Likewise, at the death of the surviving spouse, the assets in the ILIT are not included in the children's taxable estate unless they are distributed to them. Sub-trusts for **children and grandchildren** can be established under an ILIT like any other trust.

Because of the **GST leveraging** that is available to ILITs, those ILITs are often used to hold assets for generations to come. Rather than allocating the GST exemption to the death benefits, it is possible to allocate the exemption to the premium payment, which should exempt the full amount of the policy proceeds from generation-skipping tax. When used like this, ILITs are referred to as dynasty trusts. Although it is not necessary to use insurance as the funding vehicle of a dynasty trust, the leveraging of the GST exemption against the premium in ILITs is attractive to many people.

The use of joint or **survivorship life insurance** has increased over the last several decades. This type of insurance is used primarily to replace the wealth used to pay estate taxes. This type of policy insures the lives of both the husband and wife and uses the actuarial lifespan of both spouses. Accordingly, these policies are often more cost-effective than single life insurance policies. When using this type of insurance policy, the ILIT must be a joint trust that **pays out death benefits at the death of both spouses**, i.e., for the benefit of children.

ILITs can be **used in conjunction** with many other aspects of an estate plan. For example, when transferring assets to **charity** through a charitable remainder unitrust, annuity trust, or private foundation, an ILIT may be used to replace the assets given to charity. In this way, the family receives wealth through the ILIT, and the principal assets are distributed to charity free of estate tax. In sophisticated planning, the unitrust or annuity trust payments are used to fund the payment of premiums for the ILIT.

GIFTING AND ANNUAL GIFT TAX EXCLUSIONS

Q & A

Question 1: Are all gifts subject to **transfer taxation**?
Answer: No. The law provides for an annual gift tax exclusion (currently $13,000 per recipient) and a lifetime exclusion (currently $5,000,000 total).

Question 2: **What types of gifts** can be made under the law?
Answer: All types of gifts may be made, including gifts of cash, assets, tangible personal property, interests in trust, educational funds, and other rights.

Gifting of assets can accomplish many goals, including (1) helping loved ones, (2) reducing a person's taxable estate, and (3) transferring appreciating assets to a person in a lower tax bracket. Few people take advantage of the gift tax laws unless they feel that they have enough in their estates to survive the terms of their lives and truly want to see someone else enjoy the fruits of their prosperity. Nevertheless, when a gifting plan is properly implemented, both the donor and the donee receive a great benefit.

By transferring assets within the gift tax limits, a person can reduce his or her estate value at the time of death. This can be accomplished by taking advantage of the $13,000 **annual gift tax exemption** (under IRC Sec. 2503) and the $5,000,000 **lifetime gift tax exemption** (under IRC 2010).

The annual gift tax exemption can be applied to $13,000 gifts to as **many people as the donor desires each taxable year**. These gifts can either be in cash or in assets in kind. These gifts may be made up of parcels of property that may receive a valuation discount for tax purposes or undiscounted flat amounts. If a husband and wife join together in the gifts, **the exemption amount may be doubled**, i.e., $26,000 per donee annually. This is accomplished by the husband and wife each contributing $13,000 or by either of them contributing $26,000 and filing a split gift form with the spouse's 1040 tax return. It is important to remember that additional gifts may be given to individuals without limitation if the gifts are **direct transfers for the payment of educational and medical purposes**. For example, direct payments for tuition or doctor bills can be made without affecting the annual gift tax exemption.

If a gift is made that exceeds the annual gift tax exemption, a **709 gift tax return** must be filed with the person's 1040, and the lifetime gift exclusion must be allocated against the amount exceeding the annual exclusion. In the event that a person transfers more than they are allowed under his or her lifetime gift tax exemption, that person would incur a **gift tax** at the applicable transfer tax rates. As hard as it is to make a large gift and incur a gift tax, it is a very effective method of transferring wealth. The asset gifted will appreciate in the recipient's estate and escape inclusion in the donor's estate. The gift tax paid will, however, affect the donor's estate tax return. Taxable gifts made within three years of the donor's death will result in taxation in the donor's estate.

Under the 2010 Tax Relief Act, the lifetime gift tax exclusion has increased from $1 million to $5 million until 2013. This allows individuals to transfer $5 million or couples to transfer $10 million without incurring a gift tax. By making this type of transfer, large reductions to a person's taxable estate can be made; this ensures that all future growth of the asset so transferred will be outside of the donor's estate.

The amount of the gift can be increased when the value of the underlying asset being transferred is discounted. **Valuation discounts** are accepted by the IRS when the asset is a business asset subject to minority discounts, is part of a bona fide sale, or has been transferred in a properly structured trust. The amount of the discount must meet IRS scrutiny by staying within normal parameters and being part of arms length transactions. For example, gifts made through Grantor Retained Annuity Trusts, Qualified Personal Residence Trusts, Intentionally Defective Grantor Trusts, Charitable Lead Trusts, Family Limited Partnerships, and other such vehicles will receive a valuation discount. These discounts can conservatively range from 15 to 40 percent, depending on the type of vehicle used and the type of asset held in the vehicle.

Gifts specifically for education may be made through state **529 plans**. These plans, such as the Missouri Most Plan, may be established for an individual's higher education costs, including tuition, books, and lodging. The donor may gift his or her annual gift tax exclusion amount into the plan or frontload up to five years of this amount. As long as the donor does not die within the five-year period, the full amount of the gift will be excluded from the donor's taxable estate. Additionally, all of the gifts and the growth will be distributed tax free, as long as it is used for qualifying educational purposes. If the funds are not all used, the fund balance may be used for the donor's other family members' educational purposes.

SPECIAL NEEDS TRUSTS

Q & A

Question 1: Can an individual receive state or government support while retaining an estate over the **resource or income limits**?
Answer: Generally, no. If an individual has assets at his or her disposal over the resource limits, that person will be disqualified from receiving government support.

Question 2: Can a trust be established that will merely **supplement the needs** of a person receiving government support?
Answer: Depending upon who established the trust and the terms and conditions of the special needs trust instrument, the trust may escape classification as a resource for Medicaid, SSI, or veteran purposes.

Question 3: Will a special needs trust (SNT) require the trustee to **pay back** the government agencies for funds used for the benefit of the recipient?
Answer: A payback provision may be a necessary provision in the trust instrument if the trust is a self settled trust or a first party trust. Most SNTs established for a third party do not require a payback provision.

It is common for trust funds to be established for beneficiaries with special needs. These needs may be based upon the individual being **physically incapacitated, mentally disabled**, or both. In order to qualify for government assistance, this type of trust must be specially crafted and take into consideration the **requirements of such agencies** as the departments of social services and the Social Security Administration. In most cases, the availability of **Medicaid and Social Security disability** is important, and the trust must contain appropriate language that will not result in the beneficiary being disqualified from these government assistances.

The rules governing special needs trusts change from time to time and from state to state, all the while being leveraged against federal law and federal funding. It is important that the transfer of property be made in conjunction with the **local, state, and federal requirements**. The language of the trust must adhere to the regulatory requirements, or the beneficiary will not receive any government assistance. The foundational law upon which these trusts are based is found in United States Code Sec. 1396 (d) and Program Operations Manual System SI 01120.200D.2.

A special needs trust is used primarily **to supplement and not replace** the public benefits a person may receive. Such a trust may be established by the individual receiving benefits, known as a first party trust, or by someone else, known as a third party. A **first party trust** is typically established as a result of funds received by the beneficiary, for example, through a lawsuit, while a **third party trust** is typically established by a loved one for the benefit of the beneficiary. Generally, these trusts are qualifying income trusts, trusts applicable for home and community-based Medicaid waivers, and d(4)(A) and (C) trusts.

Third party trusts established by loved ones can be independent trusts and sub-trusts created within a person's revocable trust. These trusts generally require that the beneficiary has no legal authority to revoke or terminate the trust or direct the use of the funds for his or her support and maintenance. All of the trust assets must be qualified as assets beyond the reach of the beneficiary and, therefore, are **not countable resources** for Medicaid or SSI purposes.

Most special needs trust beneficiaries are endeavoring to obtain either supplemental security income (SSI) or Medicaid. **SSI** is a needs-based benefit based upon limited income and assets. A review of money received in a given month will determine eligibility. **Medicaid** in Missouri, which is known as MO HealthNet, is primarily an asset-based benefit that requires the recipient to have no more than $1,000 in assets. A review of assets, including the beneficiary's home, car, household furnishings, prepaid burial contracts, life insurance, tools, and personal items, will determine eligibility.

Special needs trusts are drafted in accordance with the criteria set forth in the *Tidrow* case, which established the criteria of **supplementing and not supplanting** the benefits granted by government agencies on behalf of the beneficiary. These trusts will limit the beneficiary's right to receive distributions according to the **trustee's absolute discretion** and the standards of disposition set forth under the trust instrument.

When establishing a special needs trust, it is important to consider who the trustee should be. On one hand, someone who has **personal knowledge** of the disabled beneficiary could have helpful input about decisions for that person's care. On the other hand, someone who understands the fiduciary requirements of administering such a trust as well as **dealing with the complicated SSI and Medicaid rules** is essential to maintaining the beneficiary's eligibility for those benefits. In many instances, an individual and corporate co-trustee arrangement may be the best solution. The ongoing trust administration must be performed in accordance with changing regulations. Therefore, the trustee must be able to comply with support and maintenance issues in a manner that will **ensure eligibility for government benefits.**

A first party special needs trust will typically include a **payback provision** that requires the trustee to repay Medicaid for funds paid on behalf of the disabled person since birth. The payback provision must also state that the repayment will be made to all states that provided medical assistance. The trust will reflect that the state is a creditor rather than a beneficiary.

Special needs trusts may be established on behalf of the disabled person under a power of attorney, by a third party, or under court order. In any instance, some type of property interest must be placed into the trust. If a third party establishes a special needs trust, that party must have a legal right to act with respect to the assets used to fund the trust.

A properly drafted special needs trust will ensure that the trust funds may be used to supplement the disabled beneficiary's needs while maintaining the beneficiary's eligibility for SSI and Medicaid.

SEPARATE VS. MARITAL PROPERTY INTERESTS: ANTENUPTIAL AGREEMENTS

Q & A

Question 1: May married couples divide their estates into **separate shares** for tax purposes?
Answer: Yes. Under Missouri law and common law jurisdictions, married parties may have separate estates for estate tax planning purposes, taking advantage of each spouse's applicable credit (basic exclusion amount).

Question 2: May either the husband or wife transfer or sell **jointly held real estate** separately?
Answer: No. The signature or waiver of both parties is required to transfer joint real estate interests.

Question 3: Is there any special creditor protection granted to spouses holding property together as joint tenants?
Answer: Yes. Under Missouri law, tenants by the entireties (spouses holding property together with rights of survivorship) property cannot be attached by an individual creditor of either party.

Question 4: Can parties considering marriage or married couples **designate by agreement** how their estates will be distributed in the event of a divorce or death?
Answer: Yes. Either a prenuptial agreement or postnuptial agreement will be upheld if the document is properly drafted, the parties have individual representation, and the assets of each spouse have been fully disclosed.

Missouri is a common law state rather than a community property state; this allows an individual **to hold separate property interests from his or her spouse**. This may be an important distinction, depending on the nature of the property interest. For example, if the asset in question was (1) received as an inheritance from parents and was understood to be eventually passed to descendants only, (2) intended to be distributed to children from a prior marriage, or (3) to be kept separate and distinct pursuant to an antenuptial agreement, then the property interest can be segregated and maintained in a separate name or in a separate trust.

Under Missouri law (R.S.Mo. Sec. 452.330), **marital property** means all property acquired by either spouse subsequent to the marriage, except for property acquired by gift, bequest, devise, descent, or property excluded by valid written agreement of the parties. Once a property interest is segregated as separate property, the appreciation occurring in the property must remain separate, or the entire interest may be tainted. Generally, the **enhancement in values** of a spouse's separate property caused by inflation and changing economic circumstances beyond the party's control is not jointly acquired property and will remain separate property. Separate property may be **transmuted or converted** into marital property by gift or by a spouse's express or implied agreement. Generally, property owned by a third party, such as an irrevocable trust, is not marital property. Additionally, compensation for non-economic damages, such as disability, is generally considered separate property. Accordingly, separate trusts funded with inheritance, disability proceeds, or those specifically addressed under an antenuptial agreement are generally free from marital attachment.

For estate planning purposes, a husband and wife under common law principles can **divide their estate** so that each may take full advantage of the federal tax exemption. Since each spouse may transfer $5 million, each spouse can establish **separate trusts funded with the basic exemption amount**. This will allow a husband and wife to transfer $10 million to their family free of estate tax. This, however, will also mean that each spouse's separate trust will be subject to seizure from their respective **creditors** and require backup insurance coverage. In the event that a husband and wife own property together as joint tenants, the couple will only be able to transfer the surviving spouse's basic exemption amount ($5 million) unless the predeceased spouse's basic exemption amount is ported over to the second spouse's taxable estate.

Separate property interests are generally only accessible by the spouse owning the interest, while joint property interests may be accessed by either spouse. Missouri law will require the **signatures of both spouses to transfer real estate** interests, while either spouse may access or transfer interests in bank accounts.

If a husband and wife hold their assets jointly as **tenants by the entireties**, neither of their separate creditors may attach their assets; only a joint judgment would be able to attach joint assets of the husband and wife. Before assets are segregated, each spouse must review the potential liability of doing so and balance that point with the benefit of saving estate taxes.

A person who inherits property may wish to **keep any inheritance separate** from his or her spouse as a precaution against a potential divorce or to ensure that the children will receive the inheritance after that person's death. This can be easily accomplished by creating an account or trust separate from a spouse. In the event that a separate trust is created, and the appreciation in the value of the trust and/or income generated from the trust is desired to be separate property, a **written agreement** between the husband and wife should be executed; such an agreement is known as an antenuptial agreement. This agreement can be made before marriage, i.e., prenuptial, or after marriage, i.e., postnuptial. In situations where there is an antenuptial agreement, the character of the property as marital or separate is not determined by the presumption of marital property set forth in the statute, but by the **terms of the contract.**

Antenuptial agreements are generally upheld under Missouri law if they are drafted correctly with separate legal representation. In order for an antenuptial agreement to be upheld, (1) each party must be represented by **separate legal counsel** to ensure that the parties understand the nature and extent of the agreement, (2) each party must **fully disclose his or her assets** to the other party to ensure realization of the extent of his or her respective waiver of rights, (3) the agreement must **cover all of the assets** and rights contemplated by the parties, and (4) the agreement must comport with the specific requirements of Missouri **law**.

Antenuptial agreements must **define the separate assets** of the husband and the wife, as well as the joint assets they may possess or intend to commingle. Each party must supply a detailed listing of his or her property and separate property with **current valuations** of the same. For example, details of cash accounts, investment accounts, real estate interests, interests in trust, business interests, retirement accounts, and tangible personal property are needed. Marital property must also be defined.

The antenuptial agreement must define what rights and property **interests are to be waived** by each party. This will require an agreement as to what interests may be transferred during life and at the death of each party. Accordingly, a recital of each party's estate plan should be incorporated into the agreement. The obligations of each party to pay **debts, taxes, and expenses** must be delineated.

If one of the party's estates is out of proportion with the other, it may be necessary for the wealthier party to make an additional contribution at the time of divorce or death to ensure that the agreement is fair and conscionable. All agreements will need to have **adequate consideration** in order to be upheld by the court.

The antenuptial agreement will need to address the rights of the parties if a petition for **dissolution of marriage** is filed; this section of the agreement may address the rights to alimony, support, and the division of property. The **residence** of the parties is an important point to be addressed in the agreement, and issues like who may reside in the marital home and who will eventually receive the home must be addressed.

If the antenuptial agreement has been drafted correctly and addresses all of the pertinent issues, and if each party has been represented by legal counsel the court will enforce its terms and conditions.

One of the recent issues facing individuals desiring to establish an estate plan is with regard to **same sex couples**. In this instance, the laws are evolving and change from state to state. For example, California, Washington, and Nevada recognize registered domestic partners (RDPs) for income tax and community property purposes. The Missouri constitution only recognizes marriage existing between a man and a woman, as does the federal Defense of Marriage Act. Accordingly, special attention must be given for planning in this context. The IRC does not grant a marital deduction to same sex couples, but each party may allocate his or her basic exemption as desired. Generally, each person must address how assets are to be owned and titled and examine the effect of the same. Beneficiary designations must be reviewed, and real estate holdings must be titled correctly to ensure that they will be managed and transferred as the party desires. This may require the creation of property agreements, powers of attorney, and other documents setting forth the individual's desires. Medical directives must be reviewed, and rights under MO HealthNet must be examined. Many times, trust agreements are established setting forth each party's rights and obligations in context with other family members.

PREDATOR AND CREDITOR PROTECTION: DISCRETIONARY AND SPENDTHRIFT TRUSTS

Q & A

Question 1: Can a trust be established that will protect a beneficiary from **lawsuits** and from persons who may try to gain access to the beneficiary's trust interest?
Answer: Yes. A trust estate may be established that protects the trust assets from the beneficiary's creditors. The trust terms may limit how the trustee distributes trust assets, taking into consideration external circumstances and complying with certain standards.

Question 2: Can trusts hold and administer business interests in a manner that will protect those interests from **creditors**?
Answer: Yes. Trusts may hold many types of assets that are themselves limited to attachment from third parties.

The distribution of assets, transfer of wealth, and avoidance of unnecessary taxes is not the only issue that must be addressed in a comprehensive estate plan; a major consideration is the protection from predators and creditors. In many instances, a person who has acquired wealth or who has inherited property may become **prey to the unscrupulous**. For example, a widow who has inherited her husband's wealth may be taken financial advantage of by a subsequent spouse, children, or third party intending to gain access to that wealth. Additionally, the unwary may hold assets in a manner that **exposes those assets** unnecessarily to creditors.

In order to protect assets from being transferred to a predator, it is most common to hold those assets in an **irrevocable trust**. This type of trust could have been created without the ability to change or revoke it, or it may have become irrevocable at the death of the settlor. This may, for example, be a marital trust, a residuary trust, a children's trust, a gifting trust, or other type of trust that does not allow the beneficiary to withdraw the principal of the trust.

In order to keep a predator from **gaining access to a trust**, the terms of the trust must state that the trustee either has absolute **discretion** to distribute assets as he or she deems proper or only pursuant to an **ascertainable standard** like health, education, maintenance, or support. In this way, a predator cannot force a beneficiary to withdraw assets from the trust. If, for example, a husband tried to gain access to a trust previously established by a predeceased spouse of his wife who did not allow encroachment of principal unless the trustee was convinced the wife had a need for health or support, no distribution would be made. Likewise, if a boyfriend of a child who had an inheritance in trust tried to gain access to the trust fund, the trustee would not make a distribution unless he or she was convinced that the child needed to be supported. In these instances, the terms and conditions of a trust for the benefit of a spouse, child, or other individual must be drafted in a manner that will stop a third party from gaining access to the trust fund.

If a settlor wishes to prevent the voluntary or involuntary attachment or transfer of assets to a creditor, a **spendthrift provision** may be inserted into the trust agreement. This type of clause will prevent a creditor from attaching trust assets while they are held in trust for the beneficiary. Other than the distribution of income for the payment of alimony, maintenance, or child support, no distribution of trust assets may be made to a creditor of the beneficiary.

Likewise, if the trust is drafted so that the trustee has absolute **discretion** to make any distribution to the beneficiary, neither the beneficiary nor the creditor can force a distribution. This is true even if the trustee's discretion is framed within an ascertainable standard like health, education, maintenance, or support.

The **avoidance of creditors** has always been an important consideration for business owners and persons conducting joint ventures. The law has acknowledges this concern and generally grants protection to those persons acting together by allowing **business associations to continue** free of creditor attachment, even when an individual owner or shareholder has a lawsuit or judgment filed against him or her. Accordingly, corporations, limited partnerships, and limited liability companies have statutorily been granted protection against the creditors of the individuals conducting business through these entities.

R.S.Mo. Chapter 351 allows one or more individuals to establish a **corporation** and to continue business operations under the requirements of the statute. The corporation is owned by its shareholders and is run by the board of directors who, in turn, elect officers who are responsible for the day-to-day affairs of the business. A corporation is established by filing articles of incorporation with the secretary of state, along with the appropriate filing fee. When the articles of incorporation are approved, a corporate charter is granted, and the business may proceed with all the benefits granted under the statute.

Corporate law is generally structured around the concept that the individual shareholders, directors, and officers are not responsible for the liabilities of the corporation. Creditors of the corporation may only attach the assets of the corporation and will not be granted a judgment against the personal assets of the shareholders, directors, or officers. Therefore, no personal liability will be assessed against the owners of the corporation unless (1) the corporation was used to perpetuate a **fraud**, (2) the corporation **charter has lapsed**, (3) the corporation did not maintain the minimum required **formalities**, or (4) the professionals of the corporation were **negligent** or acted with gross malfeasance.

The creditor protection afforded a corporation will be maintained regardless of the corporation being a **close corporation** (a small business requiring fewer formalities), an **"S" corporation** (a business granted income tax flow-through treatment under the IRC), or a **not-for-profit corporation** (a business established for charitable purposes). As long as the business is conducted within the parameters of the law, the shareholders, directors, and officers should be protected from the corporation's liabilities. A **professional corporation** (a business established to conduct professional services, e.g., accountant, attorney, physician, dentist psychologist, etc.) will not grant protection from individual creditors if the professional is liable for malpractice in the services provided. In each case, each shareholder's liability toward one another is set forth in bylaws, minutes, or a restrictive stock agreement.

Generally, each partner in a partnership is liable for the debts of the partnership. This is not the case if the partnership is formed as a limited partnership. R.S.Mo. Chapter 359 allows two or more individuals or entities to establish a **limited partnership** and to continue business operations under the requirements of the statute. A limited partnership **(LP)** is established by filing articles of partnership with the secretary of state with the appropriate filing fee. When the articles of partnership are approved, an LP charter is granted, and the enterprise may continue with all the benefits granted under the statute.

Under this arrangement, a **managing partner** is the only partner liable for business debts, while the **limited partner's** liability is limited to his or her contribution. In order to circumvent the managing partner's liability, it is common to create a limited partnership with a corporation or limited liability company as the managing partner. As long as the partnership is not used to perpetuate a fraud and is conducted for lawful purposes, the limited partners will be free of partnership liabilities.

In the event that a partner's interest is made subject to a judgment, the managing partner will receive a **"charging order"** that requires the distribution of partnership profits and expenses be made to the creditor. Accordingly, if the partnership has no net profits, no distribution will be made pursuant to the charging order. Conversely, if tax or other liability is to be transferred to a partner, it may be carried out to the creditor.

Each partner's liability toward one another is set forth in the partnership agreement. The **partnership agreement** also sets forth the restrictions each partner may have regarding the marketability of the units, the transferability of the units, the ability to liquidate units, and the control each partner has over the profits and underlying assets of the partnership.

For estate planning purposes, families will often run an enterprise together as a **family limited partnership (FLP)**. In this way, the family may establish a business relationship that will allow a centralized method of management, set forth rights and restrictions among the partners, and limit the liability of the individual partners. Because the limited partnership sets forth restrictions for the different partners, the IRC grants limited valuation discounts to the value of the partners' units. Accordingly, these types of entities are used to hold, manage, and distribute family enterprise interests in a manner that will use the state law protection afforded them, as well as the tax benefits granted under the IRC.

In an effort to combine the benefits of a corporation with the benefits of a partnership, R.S.Mo. Chapter 347 has established the use of a **limited liability company**. A limited liability company **(LLC)** is an entity established by one or more persons referred to as members. An LLC is established by filing articles of organization with the secretary of state, along with the appropriate filing fee. When the articles of organization are approved, an LLC charter is granted, and the enterprise may continue with all of the benefits granted under the statute.

An LLC is very similar to an LP; the LLC uses an operating agreement like a partnership would use a partnership agreement. All of the members' rights and responsibilities toward each other are set forth in the **operating agreement.** The operating agreement will set forth any restrictions the members may have regarding the marketability of the units, the transferability of the units, the ability to liquidate units, the control each member has over the profits, and the underlying assets of the company. The company, as a result of the statute, grants limited liability to its members. The company may have managing members and non-managing members.

For estate planning purposes, many times families will run an enterprise together as an LLC. In this way, the family may establish a business relationship that will allow a centralized method of management, set forth rights and restrictions among the members, and limit the liability of the individual members. Because the LLC sets forth restrictions for the different members, the IRC grants limited valuation adjustments to the member units. Accordingly, these types of entities are used to hold, manage, and distribute family enterprise interests in a manner that will use the state law protection afforded them, as well as the tax benefits granted under the IRC.

When establishing an estate plan, the consideration of creditor protection must be reviewed, which, in turn, requires the analysis of how estate assets are to be held and managed. As a result, the creation of a corporation, limited partnership, and limited liability company is a critical component of proper planning. Most states grant substantial creditor protection by the proper use of business entities. Nevertheless, all methods of protecting an estate from predators and creditors must be considered.

Under Missouri law, all property interests that are held between a husband and wife as **tenants by the entireties (TBE)** receive protection from each of the spouse's individual creditors. This benefit cannot be underestimated. The creditor protection granted by TBE ownership is not granted by most states, but is a strong principle under Missouri common law. Accordingly, many married clients will keep all or part of their estates in joint names. For example, the marital residence may be maintained as TBE property with the corresponding use of a beneficiary deed to later avoid probate. Additionally, the use of a joint revocable living trust by a married couple will maintain the creditor protection afforded TBE property.

Generally, qualified **retirement accounts** are exempt from creditor attachment. With regard to qualified employer plans administered under the ERISA laws, a plan participant's creditor is barred from attaching retirement plan funds. This would apply, for example, to 401(k) plans and other types of pension plans. Additionally, bankruptcy laws generally protect IRAs from seizure of creditors, with the exception of inherited accounts.

Life insurance death benefits are also generally exempt from creditor seizure, although cash values within certain limited amounts may be attached by creditors during the owner's life. If, however, the insurance policy is owned by an ILIT, the insured's creditors will not be able to attach the underlying policy, since it is held in a fiduciary capacity by the trustee of the ILIT.

As a matter of prudence and precaution, the procurement of **extra insurance** protecting the home, automobile, business, and as a general umbrella should be considered. In most instances, a creditor will first and foremost be interested in a person's insurance coverage before his or her individual assets are contemplated.

An aggressive strategy for protecting assets from creditors may involve the use of **offshore trusts.** This strategy would use an irrevocable trust that would hold all or part of an individual's assets. The assets would not be at the full control of the settlor but be distributed within the discretion of the trustee. In the event of a lawsuit or liability, the trustee or a trust protector would be required to transfer the assets to a jurisdiction indicated under the trust agreement. A jurisdiction would have been chosen that has limited obligations to honor US judgments. In many cases, a jurisdiction would be chosen that imposes a strict statute of limitations for US judgments to be filed in the foreign jurisdiction. This method may circumvent a creditor from attaching assets administered in a foreign jurisdiction. This, however, will subject the assets to laws and economies not as stable as those in the US and require a foreign trust company or trust protector to manage the assets. Additionally, some courts have held settlors in contempt if they have refused to transfer their assets back to the US. Lastly, this type of planning will necessarily incur a considerable cost to establish.

A few jurisdictions, including Missouri, have established the **statutory irrevocable spendthrift trust**. In order to circumvent the claims of a settlor's creditor, (1) the trust must be irrevocable and have a spendthrift clause, (2) the funding of the trust cannot have been fraudulent unto creditors, (3) the settlor is not the sole beneficiary of either the income or the principal of the trust, and (4) the settlor does not retain the power to amend the trust or is one of a class of beneficiaries who cannot receive a specific portion of income or principal under the trust instrument. There is no specific requirement that the trust have a Missouri trustee or that the assets be held in Missouri. Most people do not want to transfer their assets into a trust that is not at their disposal, is shared with others, or cannot be changed by them. This type of trust has various enumerations in other states such as Delaware and Alaska. It is contemplated that the Missouri asset protection legislation will be expanded in the future.

Regardless of the type of creditor protection strategies implemented, if an individual transfers property interests or establishes protective entities after he or she is aware or should be aware of a potential creditor, the non-fraudulent conveyance statute will most likely allow a creditor to undo the transfer or strategy. Therefore, it is important to establish a proper creditor strategy before a liability arises. Proactive creditor protection must be implemented, because reactive creditor avoidance will most likely fail.

ELDER CARE:
MEDICAID AND VETERAN'S BENEFITS

Q & A

Question 1: Can a trust be established that will allow a beneficiary to **receive public benefits** while also holding assets for the benefit of the beneficiary?
Answer: Yes. A special needs trust may be established for a beneficiary who is receiving government support. This type of trust must be funded and drafted properly, conforming to both the federal and state requirements.

Question 2: Can a veteran establish a trust, transfer assets to that trust, and then receive veteran's benefits?
Answer: Yes. The trust must comply with the requirements set forth by the Unites States Department of Veterans Affairs.

The practice of law known as elder care has evolved over the last several decades and specifically addresses the estate planning needs of those who are older and may have **special needs regarding their care**. As a practical matter, there is no difference in estate planning and elder planning, except that the elderly may have need of certain benefits and planning techniques that younger people may not require.

One of the most important aspects of elder care is the need to have an individual designated as the **elderly person's agent**, attorney-in-fact, representative, or trustee. In the event that a person has not been designated to make both financial and medical decisions, the probate court retains jurisdiction to appoint a conservator and a guardian for the person. The law does, however, grant many other options that should be addressed well before a person becomes elderly and may be in need of government assistance.

In order to properly plan for an elderly person's care, it is necessary to review (1) estate planning **documents**, including powers of attorney, trusts, wills, and medical directives with HIPAA releases; (2) specific **benefits** the person may be eligible to receive; and (3) **financial resources** an individual has at his or her disposal. This analysis must be done with consideration of the specific needs and desires of the elderly person. The type of environment in which to care for an elderly person is important, since that person may or may not wish to live in an extended care facility. A coordinated plan with the elderly person's family is critical in order to ensure that there is a strong support system for the person, both financially and emotionally.

Medicaid in Missouri is the federal-state system known as **MO HealthNet**. This program may provide skilled nursing coverage for elderly persons. This type of coverage is generally broken down into **medical assistance** and home- and community-based **waivers**. The details of these benefits and the granting of benefits is within the purview of the Department of Health and Human Services for the state of Missouri. The income and asset limits imposed by the statute changes periodically and must be strictly adhered to, or an elderly person may become ineligible to receive benefits or benefits may be withdrawn. In order to qualify for Medicaid, an individual must apply for the benefits and meet the needs requirements. Generally, a person may not have more than **$999.99**, and any transfer of assets within the preceding **five years** (look back) will partially disqualify the eligibility of that person for a calculated period of time.

For those elderly persons who have served in the armed forces, **veteran's benefits** may be available to them. VA benefit eligibility pertains to military service (90 consecutive days of active duty during a period of war with an honorable discharge) and must be documented for eligibility. In order to receive enhanced benefits, the claimant must (1) meet the VA's definition of **needing aid** and attendance or being **housebound**, (2) show a need for regular and ongoing **assistance** with certain activities of daily living, or (3) be

bedridden (permanently and substantially confined to his or her premises due to that person's disability). Additionally, there are financial requirements for eligibility relating to assets and income.

In order to properly care for an elderly individual, the family, especially the attorney-in-fact, must become well-educated in the eligibility requirements under Mo HealthNet, VA benefits, and the financial resources available to the individual. Assistance by a professional that specializes in this area is recommended to avoid any confusion and to ensure that all benefits are correctly made available.

Top 10 Planning Tips

1. A properly conceived estate plan will include both a trust agreement and a **pour-over will.**
2. **TOD and POD** beneficiary designation should be added to small assets in order to avoid probate.
3. **Beneficiary designations** should be made and carefully analyzed for all insurance policies, annuities, and retirement accounts.
4. All retirement plan beneficiary designations should be reviewed in order to take advantage of **spousal rollovers and stretch distributions**.
5. The use of a **revocable living trust** should always be considered in order to avoid probate, take advantage of detailed distributions for a beneficiary's interests, and tax planning.
6. An analysis of **disclaiming assets** must always be made before any trust distribution is received.
7. The use of **insurance** should always be considered in order to provide security to loved ones, liquidity for estate needs, and the reimbursement for taxes paid.
8. Transferring wealth through lifetime **gifts** may be beneficial to both the recipients and the donors.
9. **Special needs trusts** must be established if a trust beneficiary is to retain the assets for supplemental purposes and simultaneously receive government support.
10. In order to segregate assets for personal and estate planning purposes, the use of **antenuptial agreements** should be considered.

CHAPTER FOUR – ADVANCED PLANNING TECHNIQUES

For those persons who have accumulated enough wealth to result in a transfer tax having to be paid at their times of death, advanced wealth transfer planning is necessary in order **to take advantage of the tax laws** available to mitigate the situation. In this event, the process of efficiently transferring wealth is vitally important. There are numerous methods that the tax laws and trust code sanction for the transfer of wealth. The challenge is in using the **appropriate method**. This decision will depend upon the facts and circumstances presented by the settlor in light of the settlor's desires and the family dynamics surrounding the settlor's life.

The most commonly used methods of transferring wealth include the use of Family Limited Partnerships **(FLPs)**, Grantor Retained Annuity Trusts **(GRATs)**, Sales to Intentionally Defective Irrevocable Grantor Trusts **(IDIGTs)**, Qualified Personal Residence Trusts (QPRTs), Irrevocable Insurance Trusts **(ILITs)**, and charitable transfers of all types, e.g., Charitable Remainder Unitrust Trusts **(CRUTs)**, Charitable Remainder Annuity Trusts **(CRATs)**, and Private Foundations **(PFs)**. All of these methods have been sanctioned by statutes, case law, or addressed in treasury regulations or IRS private letter rulings.

It is important to remember that the fundamental reason to use these sophisticated wealth transfer methods is to **gift property interests** to other persons. These gifts are simply made within the structure of the method so chosen by the settlor. Many of these gifting methods take advantage of the **valuation discounts** that the IRS has sanctioned. In other words, at the time the gift is made, the value of the gift is adjusted so as to allow a greater gift to be made for tax purposes than would be granted at fair market value based upon certain restrictions inherent in the structure of the transaction.

FAMILY LIMITED PARTNERSHIPS

Q & A

Question 1: What is an **FLP**?
Answer: Any joint venture or business enterprise conducted by family members within the framework of a **limited partnership** is an FLP.

Question 2: How is an FLP operated?
Answer: The business will be conducted in accordance with the partnership agreement, as well as the sharing of profits and the delineation of each partner's respective interest.

As previously discussed, the use of FLPs is widespread for a number of reasons, including creditor protection, centralized management, and easy transfer of partnership interests; as an added benefit, the transfer of FLP units that are subject to restrictions will receive a reasonable valuation discount, meaning that the values of gifted units will be decreased for tax purposes. For example, if a qualified valuation expert determines that the partnership restrictions should result in the transfer receiving a 33 percent discount, the transfer of $100 of property is treated as a transfer of a $67 transfer for gift tax purposes.

In this situation, the partnership agreement must be properly drafted, setting forth the precise terms of the restrictions regarding (1) the general partner's power to **control** or liquidate the partnership and its underlying assets; (2) the limited partner's power to require the general partner to **liquidate** his or her respective shares; (3) the limited partner's power to **transfer, sell, or market** his or her interest in the partnership to third parties; and (4) the limited partner's power to require a distribution of **partnership profits and gifted interests** at the time they are made.

In using this method, an individual must establish a limited partnership with one or more other parties. The **articles of limited partnership** must be filed with the secretary of state and a charter granted. A **partnership agreement** must be prepared that sets forth the terms and conditions of the general and limited partners. **Assets**, such as real estate interests, must be transferred into the name of the partnership. Partnership units must be issued in accordance with each partner's contribution. A 709 **gift tax return** must be prepared documenting the initial transfer to the partnership and substantiating the valuation discount that was previously established by a valuation expert.

After the partnership has been established and the property has been transferred to it, the general partner must take charge of the underlying asset and **manage the interest** in a productive manner, as expected under the agreement. In the event that any partner chooses to **gift** all or any part of his or her interest to qualified recipients under the agreement, the donor must report the gift (if over the annual gift tax exclusion) on a 709 gift tax return, especially if a valuation discount is being used. The general partner must **distribute net profits** to all of the limited partners or their representatives in proportion to the respective interests. Certain **deductions** may be taken for partnership expenses, reasonable general partnership compensation, and other related fees.

For example, if a father, mother, and four children decided to enter a joint venture in order to purchase and manage a parcel of property valued at $1,000,000, they could establish an FLP to accomplish that goal. The father and mother could contribute $960,000 and each child could contribute $10,000, totaling $1,000,000. Partnership units would be issued reflecting the proportionate interests. The father, mother, or children could receive managing partnership interests, depending upon the control the parties desired to retain and in consideration of the tax and legal results of such control. Generally, the general partner's interest need only represent a small overall partnership interest, e.g., 1 to 2 percent, while the limited partner's interest would represent the remaining 98 to 99 percent of the partnership interest. After the proportionate interests have been established, each partner will have the right to receive partnership distributions in proportion to his or her respective interests. In the event that any partner desires to gift all or part of his or her interest (in accordance with the terms and conditions of the agreement), he or she may do so, taking advantage of potential valuation discounts established. The partnership agreement may require that any contribution or transfer of interests be made with a corresponding right to withdraw the value from the partnership. Accordingly, if a partner gifted $18,000 worth of partnership interests and received a 33 percent valuation discount, the tax value of the gift would equal $12,000. If a partner gifted his or her interest over a long enough period of time, that person would be able to transfer a substantial gift at a discounted rate within a structure that will ensure orderly management and protection from creditors.

GRANTOR RETAINED ANNUITY TRUSTS

Q & A

Question 1: What is a **GRAT or GRUT**?
Answer: A grantor retained annuity trust or unitrust is an irrevocable trust which is established by an individual and under which he or she retains the right to an **annuity or unitrust payment** from the trust for a specified period of time in exchange for the transfer of property to the trust. This technique is often used if the grantor has assets which are likely to increase significantly in value.

Question 2: Who receives the **trust balance** after the expiration of the payment period?
Answer: After the expiration of the payment period, the remaining balance is distributed to the designated beneficiaries, e.g., family members, outlined in the trust.

Question 3: How is the value of the **gift of the remainder** interest determined?
Answer: The gift tax value of the distribution is generally determined by subtracting the annuity or unitrust value from the distribution value, and the gift tax value is determined by actuarial and tax assumptions. If the trust value appreciates more than assumed under the government assumptions, the appreciation will escape gift taxation.

Grantor Retained Annuity Trusts (GRATs) are created pursuant to the authority granted under IRC Sec. 2702. This section of the IRC allows an individual settlor to transfer assets into a trust while

retaining an annuity interest. The trust will eventually transfer the assets to the residuary beneficiaries, e.g., family members, after the annuity has been paid to the settlor as a **gift to beneficiaries**. The value of the annuity is subtracted from the gift for tax purposes. Any **appreciation** in the trust should eventually be transferred free of gift tax.

IRC Sec. 2702 provides for special rules to determine the amount of a gift when an individual makes a transfer to a family member while the transferor retains an interest in trust. If the transfer qualifies for an exception to IRC Sec. 2702, the value of the transferor's retained interest is **subtracted** from the fair market value of the property when determining the gift tax value of the transferred interest. The value of the retained interest is determined under IRC Sec. 7520, which is **a presumed rate of growth** published by the government on a monthly basis.

For example, a parent transfers property to an irrevocable trust and retains a ten-year annuity interest that satisfies the requirements under IRC Sec. 2702. Upon the expiration of the ten-year term, the trust distributes the balance to that person's children. The amount of the parent's gift is the fair market value of the property transferred to the trust determined as of the date of such transfer less the value of the retained qualified annuity interest determined under IRC Sec. 7520.

Qualified interests are defined as (1) the right to receive a fixed amount payable at least annually, (2) the right to receive a fixed percentage of the annual fair market value of the trust property at least annually, and (3) a non-contingent remainder if all of the other interests are qualified annuity or unitrust interests. A qualified interest is one payable to the settlor for a stated term or to the settlor's estate for the balance of the term if the settlor dies.

If, under the terms of the GRAT, the settlor's estate is entitled to the balance of the annuity or unitrust payments, the actuarial value of the payments will be **includible in the settlor's gross estate**. This inclusion pertains to all property and interests the settlor had in the trust at the time of death.

Under IRC Sec. 677, a settlor is treated as the owner of a trust whose **income**, without the approval or consent of an adverse party, may be distributed to the settlor or the settlor's spouse. This is commonly referred to as a "grantor trust" for income tax purposes. A GRAT will qualify as a grantor trust, and so the income liability of the annuity payment will be taxable to the settlor. The **appreciation in the trust over the 7520 assumed growth rate**, however, will be transferred **gift tax free** to the remainder beneficiaries.

If, therefore, $1 million was transferred into a GRAT under which the settlor retained an annuity payment equal to the 7520 rate of two percent when, in fact, the assets in the trust grew at a rate of seven percent over a ten-year period, all of the appreciation in the trust could be transferred gift tax free. At the expiration of the trust term, if the trust had $350,000 remaining after making all of its annuity payments, the balance could be held or distributed to children free of transfer tax. By using this technique, a person could transfer large assets to his or her family if the assets in the trust grew at a rate substantially greater than the assumed growth rate.

SALES TO INTENTIONALLY DEFECTIVE GRANTOR TRUSTS

Q & A

Question 1: What is a sale to an **IDGT**?
Answer: An intentionally defective **grantor trust** is an irrevocable trust established by an individual under which he or she is the "grantor" for income tax purposes and remains liable for the income taxes of the trust.

Question 2: How is the IDGT funded?
Answer: The individual subsequently **sells assets** to the trust in exchange for a **promissory note** constructed under the appropriate interest rate sanctioned by the United States Treasury Department.

Question 3: What benefits do the **subsequent beneficiaries** receive after the note is paid back?
Answer: After the term of the promissory note has expired, the appreciation in the trust may be distributed to the designated beneficiaries without being subject to gift tax.

Another technique for transferring assets to family members while minimizing transfer taxes is the sale of assets to an intentionally defective grantor trust **(IDGT)**. In overview, a person creates a trust for the benefit of children but retains certain specific and limited powers over the trust. Once the trust has been created, the **settlor sells assets to the trust** in exchange for a long-term **installment note**. In so doing, the settlor of the trust has converted an appreciating asset into an asset with a fixed value, i.e., the promissory note. The sales transaction is entered into at fair market value, so the sale by the settlor does not result in a gift to his or her children. The settlor will not be subject to income tax on the sale of the assets to the trust, because the trust qualifies as a "grantor trust" for income tax purposes and the sale is legally **a sale to him or her**.

The settlor is treated as the trust owner for income tax purposes but not for estate tax purposes. This allows for the sale of the assets by the settlor to the trust to avoid capital gains; furthermore, the interest on the promissory note received by the settlor will **avoid being subjected to income taxes**. **Appreciation** on the assets sold to the trust grows **outside of the settlor's estate**. If the settlor dies before the note has been paid in full, only the **unpaid balance due on the note is included in the settlor's estate.**

The only gift element of this transaction arises from the requirement that the trust be **capitalized** or seeded with sufficient assets (other than the property received from the sale in exchange for the note) to establish the independence of the trust from the assets purchased from the settlor. The capitalization is generally 10 to 15 percent of the value of the installment note, so there is a **debt to equity ratio** of at least ten to one. It is important that the trust has independent equity so that the note owed the settlor is not re-characterized as an equity interest which would, in turn, bring inclusion into the settlor's estate. The seed monies contributed to the IDGT will **constitute a gift**, because this contribution is not part of the sale and the note payment has no applicability to it. Accordingly, the settlor's gift tax credit will need to be used against the seed fund, and a 709 gift tax return will need to be filed. In order to provide further security for the note obligation, the trust beneficiaries could provide personal guarantees for the payment of the note.

The IDGT is structured as a "grantor trust" for income tax purposes, and so the settlor is typically granted the power, exercisable in a non-fiduciary capacity, to reacquire trust property by **substituting other property** of an equivalent value. Where the power of substitution is used as the "defective" retained interest, the settlor should never be named as the trustee.

As the **settlor pays income tax** on the trust income, such payment reduces the settlor's own taxable estate by the amount of the tax paid. The settlor's payment of the income tax on the trust allows the trust to effectively accumulate income on a "tax free basis." This may be viewed as the settlor making a transfer tax free addition to the trust for purposes of both the gift tax and generation-skipping transfer tax.

Since the IDGT is **out of the settlor's taxable estate**, the trust could be used to purchase life insurance on the life of the settlor. If the return on the trust assets exceeds the note obligations and the trust is properly capitalized, the excess income may be used to **purchase a life insurance policy** on the settlor's life. When the IDGT has paid off the note and the balance is held or transferred to the remaining beneficiaries, the life insurance policy would also transfer, resulting in a large windfall to the remaining beneficiaries at the settlor's death.

The **installment note** generally provides for payments over a specified term of years. It is recommended that the selected duration of the note be within the life expectancy of the settlor, as this provides further economic substance to the transaction. The note typically provides for the payment of **interest only during the term, with a balloon** principal payment due at the end of the designated term. The note may be structured around the rates applicable under IRC Secs. 7872 and 1274. These rates for note obligations are more favorable than the 7520 rate.

If the **settlor should die** before the installment note has been satisfied, the remaining interest payment should be classified as income in respect of a decedent (IRD), because the grantor status will have ended upon the death of the settlor. The initial design of the IDGT is structured to retain enough power to render the settlor taxable on the trust income but not enough power to allow the trust property to be included in the settlor's estate.

For example, if we assume a settlor created an irrevocable trust and sold $1 million of assets to the trust in exchange for an installment note of $1 million bearing a 7872 rate of two percent payable over a five-year period, and if we further assume the assets of the trust appreciated at a rate of seven percent, then all of the appreciation over the two percent would later be transferred to the remaining beneficiaries gift tax free after the note had been satisfied. If the trust had been capitalized with $100,000, this would be deemed a gift, and the settlor's gift tax credit would need to be allocated against it.

Then, at the end of the note term, the note would be paid in full and the remaining balance held or distributed to the remaining beneficiaries. If the trust had purchased life insurance on the life of the settlor, the death benefit would be paid to the beneficiaries free of transfer tax. By using this technique, a person could transfer large assets to his or her family if the assets in the trust grow at a rate substantially greater than the note obligation.

Comparison of GRATS and IDGTs

Comparing the installment sale to a defective grantor trust technique with GRAT technique results in an arguably more favored position for the IDGT technique, since, unlike the GRAT, the IDGT is not specifically **authorized by statute.**

In the case of the GRAT, if the grantor dies during the term of the retained interest, all of the **trust property is included** in the grantor's estate at its then fair market value, obviously including any post-transfer appreciation. In the case of the installment sale to the IDGT, survivorship to any specific term is not required. While the GRAT is subject to a mortality risk, the installment sale to the IDGT is not subject to such a risk. Only the value of the **unpaid balance of the installment note is included** in the grantor's estate in the case of the IDGT. Post-sale appreciation escapes estate tax.

Another advantage of the installment sale of the IDGT over the GRAT is that the required interest rate used in the installment sale transaction will be lower than the rate used for a GRAT. A **lower interest rate** reduces the amount to be repaid to the grantor and correspondingly increases the amount that is passed to the beneficiaries without being taxed to the grantor.

Where there is a desire to involve grandchildren as trust beneficiaries, the installment sale to the IDGT is the preferred vehicle. If a GRAT is used for this purpose, the **generation-skipping transfer tax exemption** may not be allocated until the end of the initial term of the trust, since this initial term constitutes the estate tax inclusion period (ETIP), which is any period in which the trust would be included in the grantor's estate if the grantor were to die.

In the case of the GRAT, the payment schedule to the grantor must be established at the inception of the trust. **Property cannot be added to the GRAT** once it has been created and funded. The GRAT payments are fixed by the trust documents and are therefore inflexible. Each year's annuity payment may not exceed 120 percent of the amount paid in the preceding year. To the extent that the GRAT does not produce sufficient income to cover the required annuity payments, it is possible that the trust will have to return principal to the grantor to satisfy the annual payment obligation.

The GRAT is expressly forbidden from using a **promissory note** for the payment of an annuity. Conversely, the installment sale is typically structured as an interest-only note with a balloon principal payment due at the end of the term. The trust (and its beneficiaries) are able to derive the benefit of the earnings and the growth of the unpaid deferred principal free of any income tax liability. Less money is returning to the grantor when the IDGT technique is used. If desired, additional gifts or sales can be made to the IDGT at any time. If funds are needed by the grantor before they become due in accordance with the payment schedule of the note, a right held by the trustee to prepay the note without penalty can address this issue.

When the GRAT is used, **no one other than the grantor of the trust can participate** in the trust until the end of the retained interest term. No similar restrictions apply in the case of a trust that acquires an installment note such as the IDGT. The trust beneficiaries can receive trust distributions or otherwise enjoy the trust property at any time.

In the case of *Walton v. Commissioner*, 115 TC 589 (2000), Walton held that a zeroed-out GRAT was possible; hence, in those circumstances where it is feasible to construct a zeroed-out GRAT, the GRAT and the IDGT can both be created free of **gift tax liability**. The IRS announced, in its acquiescence cited above, that it would revise its GRAT regulations to conform to the tax court's decision.

Another advantage that favors the use of a GRAT is **certainty of tax treatment**. Section 2702 and the regulations thereunder provide specific statutory authority and rather detailed guidance in how to structure the transaction in a manner that will qualify it as a GRAT without any doubt. The installment sale to the IDGT does not enjoy such published clarity. There is no IRC section and no definitive pronouncement from the IRS specifically authorizing the use of this technique, although IRS ruling 2004-64 is a significant step in providing at least some comfort that, when properly structured, the defective trust technique is viable.

QUALIFIED PERSONAL RESIDENCE TRUSTS

Q & A

Question 1: What is a **QPRT**?
Answer: A qualified personal residence trust is an irrevocable trust established by an individual and under which he or she transfers his or her residence to a trust for a term of years and retains **the right to reside in the residence**. The specified term of years retained under the trust instrument will determine the actuarial and tax value of the retained right.

Question 2: What happens to the **home after the expiration of the settlor's term** to reside in the home?
Answer: After the expiration of the residency term, the **home will be distributed to the designated beneficiaries.**

Question 3: What is the **value of the gift** to the remainder beneficiaries?
Answer: The value of the **gift** of the home will be determined by subtracting the gift tax value of the retained right to reside in the home from the fair market value of the home when it was transferred into the trust. Generally, any **appreciation** in the value of the home

that exceeds the government's assumed growth rate will escape gift taxation.

Question 4: May the settlor remain in the residence after the expiration of the residency term?
Answer: Yes, if the settlor pays fair market rent to the trustee of the QPRT.

A qualified personal residence trust **(QPRT)** is an irrevocable trust that holds an interest in one personal residence of the settlor, along with other related assets such as cash for expenses and/or sales proceeds from the sale of the residence. A QPRT must comply with the requirements set forth in IRC Sec. 2702 and Reg. Sec. 25.2702-5(c). When a person **gifts his or her residence** to a QPRT, that person makes a gift to his or her descendants but retains the right to reside and **occupy the residence for a certain period of time** called the trust term. When the trust term expires, the ownership of the residence passes to the remaining beneficiaries designated under the trust instrument.

A QPRT will typically provide that if the **settlor dies** before the end of the QPRT term, the trust terminates and the **residence reverts** to the settlor's estate. The remainder beneficiaries receive the trust property only at end of the term and will not receive it if the settlor dies prior to that time. In the event that a **beneficiary dies** prior to the end of the trust term, most QPRTs provide that the deceased child's share lapses, thereby increasing the other children's share. QPRT shares that are distributed to a deceased child's descendants may incur generation-skipping transfer tax problems, because the GST exemption cannot be allocated against the trust until the term has expired.

Based upon the current gift tax system, and if housing prices are increasing, the gift of a settlor's residence to a QPRT is a tax bargain for the settlor. This is because the settlor receives a **valuation discount** in computing the value of his or her gift based upon the interest that is retained by the settlor. If the settlor survives the trust term, the entire value of the residence is excluded from that person's estate, and the settlor only paid gift tax on a discounted valuation of the residence. However, if the settlor dies during the trust term, the residence comes back into his or her estate, resulting in no tax savings and with the settlor's estate in the same position as it would have been had the transfer of the residence not been made.

The QPRT is a tax-favored method of making use of an individual's gift tax exemption and is generally a safe harbor technique that works especially well in environments of high interest rates. The QPRT does not depend upon the investment within it achieving a particular investment return and will be effective even if the residence value remains stagnant.

For example, if an individual has four children and a residence valued at $1 million, a gift of the residence can be made to a QPRT. The trust may provide that the settlor continues to live in the residence free of rent for a 15-year term. During the trust term, the settlor may be the trustee of the trust and will be required to use the residence and pay all of the expenses associated with its upkeep. If the settlor decides to sell the residence, the proceeds of the sale will be kept in the trust. The trustee could take the sales proceeds and purchase another residence or invest the proceeds for the balance of the term and pay the settlor a cash annuity. At the end of the term, the four children will become beneficial owners under the trust, even if the settlor continues as the trustee. The settlor will have the option to continue to live in the residence and pay rent to the trustee as a tenant of the trust. The rent will flow through the trust to the children as the beneficiaries and further decrease the settlor's estate. When the trust was funded, the settlor filed a 709 gift tax return showing the value of the gift at approximately one half of the $1 million fair market value of the residence. The amount of the gift will vary, depending upon the trust term and the current federal discount rate. If the value of the gift is less than the settlor's remaining lifetime gift tax exemption, no gift tax will be due. If the settlor dies during the trust term, the residence would revert back to the settlor's estate. Accordingly, the settlor may have made other arrangements for the children, e.g., purchasing insurance payable to the children during the trust term. If a child died during the trust term, the remaining children would receive the residence. Accordingly, the settlor may have made other arrangements for the descendants of a deceased child, e.g., purchasing insurance on the child's life.

Generally, a QPRT cannot allow the prepayment of the annuity payment if the residence has been sold and the investment is being paid to the settlor as a GRAT. The reimbursement for income taxes is also generally not allowed under the trust instrument. It is generally not advised to transfer mortgaged property into a QPRT, because the mortgage payments constitute an additional gift to the trust. The trust should, however, allow the instrument to be amended in order to comply with the current regulations.

If the QPRT is structured correctly, the residence will have been gifted to the settlor's children at a discounted value, resulting in little or no gift tax having been paid. The settlor may then be able to transfer more wealth to his or her children through the payment of rent (subject to income tax to the children). If the settlor decides to undo the QPRT gifts, purchases and reverse QPRTs are available but costly and complex in nature.

GIFTING AND CHARITABLE DEDUCTIONS

Q & A

Question 1: Why should **charitable gifting** be integrated into an estate plan?
Answer: Charitable gifts will help continue **philanthropic** purposes.

Question 2: What tax benefits are derived from charitable gifts?
Answer: If properly structured, charitable gifts will grant **tax deductions** (income, gift, and estate) to the individual making the gift.

Charitable gifting is important to many people as both a method of helping those in need and a way of obtaining a charitable tax deduction. The federal and state laws generally grant income, gift, and estate tax deductions for transfers to or for the benefit of a **qualified charitable organization**. These types of organizations are generally defined under IRC Sec. **501(c)(3) and 170(1)(B)** as organizations operated exclusively for charitable, scientific, educational, literary, or religious purposes. Gift and estate tax deductions may be received under IRC Sec. 2522 (a) and 2055 (a).

The amount of the **charitable deduction** an individual receives is subject to **percentage limitations** and depends upon the donor's income, and whether the organization is a private foundation or a public charity. Contributions given to either a private foundation or a public charity that exceed the percentage limitations in the year of the gift are generally subject to a five-year carryover, although any unused carryover is lost upon the donor's death.

Public charities generally enjoy a broad base of public support. The income tax charitable deduction for gifts to public charities of cash and ordinary income property is generally limited to **50 percent** of the donor's contribution base, i.e., the donor's adjusted gross income or AGI. Generally, the income tax charitable deduction for a gift to a public charity of long-term capital gain property is limited to **30 percent** of the donor's adjusted gross income.

A **private foundation** is a charitable organization that has been established by an individual donor or family. The income tax charitable deduction for gifts of cash or ordinary income property to private foundations is limited to **30 percent** of the donor's AGI in the year of contribution. The income tax charitable deduction for a gift of long-term capital gain property to a private foundation is generally limited to **20 percent** of a donor's AGI in the year of the contribution.

IRC Sec. 2055(a) allows an **estate tax charitable deduction**, while IRC Sec. 2522(a) allows a **gift tax charitable deduction** for transfers to 501(c)(3) organizations. None of the percentage and valuation limitations on the income tax charitable deduction under IRC Sec.170 apply to the estate or gift tax charitable deduction. Accordingly, the gift and estate tax charitable deductions are unlimited, as long as the property gifted was included in the decedent's gross estate.

Charitable gifts may also qualify for gift and estate tax charitable deductions if they are structured properly in a split-interest trust. A **split-interest trust** is a gift in which a charitable beneficiary and a noncharitable beneficiary share interests in the same property. In this case, the charitable deduction will not be allowed for transfers to a trust that has both a charitable and a noncharitable beneficiary, unless the trust meets certain requirements for split-interest trusts. In order to meet the requirements under IRC Sec. 2055(e)(2) and 2522(c)(2), gift and estate tax charitable deductions are allowed for (1) the remainder interest in a charitable remainder annuity trust **(CRAT)**, a charitable remainder unitrust **(CRUT)**, or a pooled income fund; (2) the income interest in a charitable lead annuity trust **(CLAT)** or a charitable lead unitrust **(CLUT)**; and (3) the non-trust remainder interest in a personal residence or a farm.

Unless a charitable organization qualifies as a publicly supported organization or a church, it will generally be classified as a **private foundation**. Contributions to a private foundation will qualify for a charitable gift tax deduction if made during the donor's lifetime or a federal estate tax deduction if made at a donor's death. Unlike the estate and gift charitable deduction, the donor's income tax charitable deduction for gifts to a private foundation during his or her life is subject to percentage limitations.

Private foundations are subject to several **complex operating rules and restrictions** that do not apply to public charities. Failure to follow these rules and restrictions may result in additional taxes and penalties. There are several prohibited acts in which a private foundation may not engage.

Many individuals may wish to make charitable transfers or bequests through a fund, which is simple and easy and will accomplish their specific charitable goals. In this instance, the use of a **donor-advised fund** may be beneficial. A donor-advised fund is a separate fund, but not a separate entity, within a public charity. The donor's contributions are accounted for within the public charity's records, and the donor is permitted to "name" a fund after himself or herself or a family member. The public charity must control the gift in all respects, including the right to control investments and control the disposition of the donated funds for charitable purposes. The donors or their designees generally maintain the privilege of making non-binding recommendations to the governing body as to which charities should receive grants from their particular funds. With a donor-advised fund, control is sacrificed, because the donor's recommendations are advisory only, and the right to advise is generally limited by the lifespans of the advisors or their designees.

Many public charities have established **charitable gift annuities** that allow an individual to make a gift to the charity and receive both a charitable deduction and a current stream of annuity payments. A charitable gift annuity is a contract between a donor and a charity in which the donor transfers money or other property to a charity in exchange for the charity's promise to pay the beneficiary a fixed dollar amount each year for the beneficiary's lifetime. The annuity may be a single life annuity or a joint and survivor annuity, and payments may be annual or more frequent. The annuity payment may be either immediate or deferred. The amount of the annuity payment is generally used as recommended by the committee of gift annuities and depends on the age of the beneficiary. The annuity rates are typically conservative, so the charity receives a significant benefit from the transaction while minimizing the possibility that the charity will be required to use its own finds to make the payments.

A **pooled income fund** is another type of split-interest gift that is structured under the IRC. A donor transfers money or securities to a separately maintained fund created by a public charity, where it is invested with gifts from other donors. The donor retains an income interest for life but makes a gift of the remainder interest. The donor, in turn, receives a pro rata share from the funds earnings each year for the rest of his or her life.

CHARITABLE REMAINDER TRUSTS

Q & A

Question 1: What is a **CRUT or CRAT**?
Answer: A charitable remainder unitrust or charitable remainder annuity trust are both **irrevocable trusts** established by an individual under which he or she retains the right to either a **unitrust or annuity** payment for a specified period.

Question 2: How is a CRT funded, and who receives the benefit from the trust?
Answer: The individual transfers assets into the trust and designates a **charity as the beneficiary** after his or her interests have expired.

Question 3: What are the **tax benefits** of setting up a CRT?
Answer: Appreciated assets can be transferred and sold within the CRT without immediate taxation. After the individual has transferred property into the trust, the value of the future distribution to the charity is determined by using the government's assumed actuarial and growth rates. The individual will receive an **income tax deduction** for the value of the gift of the future distribution.

Generally, the value of the charitable distribution will receive an **estate tax deduction.**

The use of making charitable gifts through a charitable remainder trust, i.e., **CRT**, is a very popular technique. In using this technique, an individual may transfer assets into a CRT, receive a qualified payment, and later distribute the balance to a qualified charity.

A CRT allows an individual, referred to as the donor, to donate assets to a charity while retaining an interest in the donated assets or providing another individual or entity with an interest in the donated assets for a specified period of time. The donor transfers property to an **irrevocable trust** that provides for the noncharitable beneficiary of the CRT to receive a stream of **payments for a specified period of time**. At the expiration of the period, the remaining assets will be transferred to the charitable beneficiary. Accordingly, a CRT is a split-interest gift, because both a charitable beneficiary and a noncharitable beneficiary receive interest in the same property. The donor will receive an income tax deduction and a gift tax charitable deduction or an estate tax deduction based upon the present value of the remainder interest ultimately passing to charity. A charitable deduction is allowed only if the noncharitable interest is in the form of an annuity interest or a unitrust interest, which must be fixed and may not change over time.

CRTs are subject to certain rules in order for them to not be disqualified. These rules and requirements include the following: (1) **no distributions for emergencies** or other purposes may be made from a CRT; (2) the annuity or unitrust payment must be **prorated** in the case of a short taxable year other than the final year; (3) the CRT must include language that directs the trustee to **correct improper distributions** made or not made due to the incorrect valuation of the CRT assets; (4) interim distributions to charities may be permissible if within certain parameters; and (5) the amount paid must be equal to at least **5 percent but not more than 50 percent** of the initial fair market value of the assets of the trust. The present value of the remainder interest that passes to charity must equal at least **10 percent** of the initial fair market value of the assets contributed to the trust. If the CRAT or CRUT fails any of these tests, the trust will be disqualified and the charitable deduction voided.

CRATs pay a defined annuity, either **a fixed dollar amount or a fixed percentage** of the initial fair market value, regardless of the value of the trust assets or the income generated by the trust. CRUTs pay a defined percentage of the net fair market value of the assets of the trust valued as of a certain day each year to the noncharitable beneficiary, at least annually. This amount is referred to as the "**unitrust amount**." The unitrust amount fluctuates, even though the defined percentage is fixed. Therefore, unlike a CRAT, a CRUT cannot be exhausted by distribution to the noncharitable beneficiary, because the unitrust amount will decrease as the value of the assets of the trust decreases.

There are several variations of CRUTs that the IRS has approved. A variation of the CRUT, called **a net income CRUT**, is a CRUT that pays the noncharitable beneficiary the lesser of the income of the trust or the unitrust amount. The IRC allows a net income CRUT to include a **"makeup" provision**, specifying that deficits between the required unitrust amount that would otherwise have been payable and the net income of the CRUT shall be made up in later years. This makeup is to be made to the extent that the CRUT income in those later years exceeds the required unitrust amounts for such later years. A CRUT with a makeup provision is referred to as a "**NIMCRUT**."

The IRC regulations also allow a CRUT that uses either the net income or net income with a makeup provision to pay out using those methods for an initial period to later **"flip"** to a standard CRUT, i.e., the fixed unitrust amount, for the balance of the term. The flip must be triggered by a specific date or by a specific event, and the date or event is not to be at the discretion of the trustee or any other person. The triggering date or event could be, for example, the sale of unmarketable securities, the death or birth of an individual, or the marriage or divorce of an individual.

If the noncharitable beneficiary is an individual, then **the term of the CRT** may be for either the duration of the beneficiary's life or for not more than 20 years. If the noncharitable beneficiary is not an individual, then the term of the CRT must be for a term of years not to exceed 20 years. If the CRT will hold **unmarketable assets**, the trust will not qualify for an income, gift, or estate deduction unless an independent trustee values the unmarketable assets or, alternatively, the value is determined by a **qualified appraisal** from a qualified appraiser.

If the CRT has been structured properly, an **income tax deduction** will be available for the actuarial value of the charity's remainder interest determined under IRC Sec. 7520. CRTs themselves are generally exempt from income taxes. Distributions to noncharitable beneficiaries of the CRT carry out the CRT's **income to the beneficiaries**, where it is taxed to the beneficiaries on a tier basis. The purpose of the tier system is to ensure that income taxed at the highest rate is distributed to the beneficiary before distributions taxed at a lower rate. Therefore, under the **tier system**, distributions will be taxed as ordinary income, then capital gains, then other income, and lastly as a return of capital.

If the CRT is established during the donor's life, the donor is entitled to a **charitable gift tax deduction** for the actuarial value of the charity's remainder interest. A transfer to a CRT in which the donor retains the annuity or unitrust interest does not have any gift tax consequences, i.e., the only gift is the gift of the remainder interest that qualifies for the gift tax charitable deduction. If the donor gives annuity or unitrust payments to another person, gift tax may be imposed.

The remainder beneficiary must be an organization described in IRC Sec. 2055(a) and 170(c) in order to qualify for the estate tax deduction. If the donor is a beneficiary of the CRT, then the CRT will be included in the donor's gross estate; however, an **estate tax charitable deduction** will be available for the remainder interest going to charity.

It is possible to **transfer retirement accounts** and assets classified as income in respect of a decedent (IRD) to a CRT. If an individual wishes to make a charitable bequest, making a gift of IRD to a charity, this can be done through a CRT, and income taxes can be saved. The trustee of a CRT established under an individual's will or revocable living trust (RLT) may be named as the primary beneficiary of that individual's retirement account or IRA. In this instance, the CRT does not realize income upon receipt of the proceeds because the CRT is tax exempt. There is no gift tax as long as the beneficiary designation remains revocable. The decedent's estate will receive an unlimited estate tax charitable deduction for the actuarial value of the remainder interest in the CRT.

For example, if an individual created a CRUT and transferred $1 million of low-basis stock into the CRT at 65 years of age and retained the right to receive a five percent unitrust payment for life designating his or her favorite 501(c)(3) charity, the following results would occur: (1) the stock could be sold without immediate recognition of capital gains, because the CRT is a tax-exempt entity; (2) the donor/settlor will receive a current charitable income tax deduction in the approximate amount of $448,181, which can be carried forward for five years; (3) the settlor, as the unitrust recipient, will receive taxable distributions in the form of the unitrust payment under the four-tier system of taxable distributions; and (4) eventually, when the term of the unitrust distribution has expired, the charity will receive the balance in the trust, and the settlor's estate will receive an estate tax deduction for the amount being distributed to the charity.

CHARITABLE LEAD TRUSTS

Q & A

Question 1: What is a **CLAT or CLUT**?
Answer: A charitable lead annuity trust or charitable lead unitrust are **irrevocable trusts** that are established by an individual under which he or she grants a charity the right to receive either an annuity payment or a unitrust payment for a specified period of time.

Question 2: What does a charity receive out of a CLAT or CLUT?
Answer: The individual transfers assets into the trust, and the designated **charity receives the payment** i.e., "lead interest" until the term expires.

Question 3: Who receives the balance in the CLAT or CLUT?
Answer: After the payment term has expired, the remaining balance will be distributed to the **designated remainder beneficiaries**, e.g., children of the donor. Generally, the appreciation in the trust after the charity has receives all of its payments will escape gift taxation.

A charitable lead trust **(CLT)** is another type of split-interest gift, because both a charitable and a noncharitable beneficiary receive interest in the same property. In this type of arrangement, the donor transfers property to an irrevocable trust that pays the designated charity a stream of payments **(the lead amount)** for a specified period of time. At the end of the specified period, the settlor may reclaim his or her interest or provide for the assets to be transferred to a noncharitable beneficiary.

A charitable deduction is allowed only if the charitable interest is in the form of an annuity or unitrust interest. Accordingly, a CLT may be established as a charitable lead annuity trust **(CLAT)** or a charitable lead unitrust **(CLUT)**.

A CLT may be established for a term of years or for the life of one or more individuals who are living at the time the CLT is created. There is no limit on the number of years a CLT may operate; there is, however, a limit as to whose lives may be used to determine the CLT term.

To obtain an **income tax deduction**, the settlor must be treated as the owner of the lead interest for purposes of the grantor trust rules, i.e., the CLT must be a **grantor trust** as defined under the IRC. In this instance, the income of the CLT will be taxed to the settlor, even though the lead interest is being distributed to a charitable beneficiary. This will allow greater assets to accumulate in the CLT but will require the settlor to be able to bear the income tax burden.

On the other hand, a **non-grantor trust** is not a grantor trust under the IRC, so the income of the CLT is not taxed to the grantor. A non-grantor trust is taxed as a separate entity with the income taxable to the trust. A CLT is not exempt from income tax but will receive an income tax deduction for the income distribution to the charity each year. The character of payments made to charitable beneficiaries is not determined by the tier system for income tax purposes. There are no percentage limitations on the amount of income that a CLT can deduct for payments made to charity.

The charitable gift or estate tax deduction allows a donor to obtain a discount in the value of the gift to the remainder beneficiaries, e.g., children. If the CLT is established during the settlor's life, the settlor is entitled to a **charitable gift tax deduction** for the value of the charity's interest upon the creation of the trust. If the remainder beneficiaries are individuals other than the settlor, e.g., children, the value of the remainder interest is a gift that is subject to gift tax when the trust is created. The remainder beneficiaries, however, will receive the balance in the trust without additional gift tax.

It is possible to create a CLAT with a charitable interest equal to the entire value of the property transferred to the trust. In this case, the value of the remainder interest, which is the interest gifted to the noncharitable beneficiaries, would equal zero, referred to as a "**zeroed-out CLAT**." In this instance, no gift would be made to the remainder beneficiaries, e.g., children, even if they received a substantial amount at the termination of the trust, due to the trust assets appreciating beyond anticipation.

If a CLAT is structured so that the remainder beneficiaries are grandchildren or skipped persons as defined for GST tax purposes, the distribution will be **subject to GST tax**. This is because the determination of the GST exemption cannot be made or allocated until the end of the trust period, since the current asset values must be used; since this cannot be determined, the GST tax exemption cannot be allocated. As a result, CLATs are customarily structured to distribute to living children only.

For example, if a 65-year-old man sets up a CLAT, funds it with $1 million, and names his favorite charity as the recipient of an annuity payment equal to five percent of the trust value for ten years with a current approved federal rate (AFR) equal to 2.8%, thereafter naming his son as the remainder beneficiary after the annuity has been paid to the charity, the following results will occur: (1) the CLAT will pay the charity approximately $435,375 over the ten-year period; (2) the CLAT will pay income taxes on the income and gains in the trust because it is not a tax-exempt entity; (3) the settlor will not have to pay any gift taxes but will have to allocate his or her gift tax exclusion of approximately $564,625 against the value eventually gifted to his son after the annuity has been paid to the charity; and (4) upon the completion of the payment of the annuity to the charity, the trustee will distribute the balance of the trust to the settlor's son free of transfer tax.

PRIVATE FOUNDATIONS

Q & A

Question 1: What is a **private foundation**?
Answer: A private foundation is either a trust or a corporation established for charitable or **philanthropic purposes**. The foundation is established by a group of individuals in order to receive funds which will then be distributed to other charities for charitable purposes or to enable other charitable works.

Question 2: Is a private foundation **tax exempt**?
Answer: Yes. After the foundation has filed a form 1023 for its **tax exemption**, donors may receive an appropriate deduction for gifts made to it during life and at death.

A private foundation may be created and organized as a charitable **trust or as a not-for-profit corporation**. If the corporate entity is used, **articles** of incorporation must be filed with the secretary of state in order to obtain its charter. In this case, a board of directors must be composed of at least three persons. **Bylaws** must be drafted that set forth the duties of the officers and directors. The articles, bylaws, and corporate minutes must be aligned with the charitable requirements set forth under the IRC. The foundation should have an **operating agreement** demonstrating compliance with the IRC and corresponding regulations. After this has been done, the trust or corporation must file a **form 1023** with the IRS to obtain recognition of its tax-exempt status. The form 1023 will request extensive information regarding the financial structure of the organization and a detailed explanation of the foundation's purposes. All of the foundation's documentation must be aligned with the general restrictions imposed against foundations.

A private foundation is subject to several restrictions: (1) A private foundation may not engage in **self-dealing** with any person or organization that might be classified as a "disqualified person" in relation to the private foundation. A "disqualified person" includes substantial contributors, i.e., the creator, managers, family members, and other entities which are under more than 20 percent control of such persons. (2) An **excise tax** of 2 percent is imposed each year on the net investment income of a private foundation. This tax may be reduced to 1 percent if the foundation makes sufficiently large distributions to public charities. (3) A private foundation is required to make **qualifying distributions for each taxable year equal to five percent** of the net fair market value of the foundation's assets; this does not include assets used to carry out the foundation's charitable purposes. In general, qualifying distributions include any amount paid to accomplish exempt purposes. Charitable distributions in excess of the amount required to be distributed for a given year generally reduce the required distribution in subsequent years. (4) A private foundation that owns more than 2 percent of the outstanding stock of any company may be subject to restrictions on **excess business holdings**. (5) Generally, the law imposes a tax on high-risk investments referred to as "**jeopardy investments**" on the assumption that these types of investments jeopardize the carrying out of the exempt purposes of the foundation. Some examples are trading stock on margin, trading in futures, investing in oil and gas wells, the purchase of puts and calls, and selling short. (6) A private foundation is generally subject to a 10 percent tax on the amount of a **taxable expenditure**, which is a payment by the foundation other than a qualifying distribution or payment of taxes and expenses.

A private foundation must also file **form 990-PF** annually with the IRS. Form 990-PF reports income earned, includes details of the foundation's expenses of operation, lists charitable grants made, and lists names and addresses of the foundation's directors and officers, and lists details on the foundation's activities.

A private foundation can be structured as a "**supporting foundation**," also known as a conduit or pass-through foundation. In this instance, the foundation takes advantage of the more liberal limitations on the charitable income tax deduction applicable to gifts made to public charities, because all contributions flow through to the public foundation of which the foundation is a conduit. This special exception is conditioned upon all the contributions being made and distributed by the conduit foundation within certain time limits each year.

Another variation of a private foundation is an "**operating foundation**," which is a private foundation subject to the applicable restrictions and reporting requirements that must directly carry out its charitable programs instead of making grants to other organizations. In this instance, there is also the requirement that to qualify as an operating foundation, the foundation must expend substantially all of its net investment income directly for the active conduct of its exempt activities.

For example, an individual could establish a not-for-profit corporation with at least three board members with the secretary of state. Bylaws, minutes, and an operating agreement could be established demonstrating the corporation's operations as a private foundation in compliance with the US Department of the Treasury rules and IRS regulations. The foundation could complete the form 1023 and receive its tax exemption, and the following would occur: (1) the foundation would operate as a tax-exempt entity under the IRS regulations and distribute 5 percent of its income each year to other charitable endeavors or entities; (2) donors could receive an income tax deduction for contributions to the foundation and an estate tax deduction for distributions at death to the foundation; (3) the board members may receive a modest salary for running the foundation, depending upon the value of the fund and the amount of time required to perform their duties; and (4) the foundation would continue to support charitable endeavors pursuant to its articles and the charitable aspirations of the founding board until its funds are exhausted.

Top 10 Planning Tips

1. Business ventures conducted with family members can be managed effectively through the use of **family limited partnerships**. In this way, creditor protection may be taken advantage of and management may be centralized. The distribution of partnership interests is an easy method of organizing and distributing business assets, profits, and rights.
2. **Gifts of the appreciation on assets** may be made to designated beneficiaries through a trust, after the settlor has received an annuity or unitrust interest, with a gift tax adjustment through the use of a **GRAT**.
3. **Gifts of the appreciation on assets** may be made to designated beneficiaries through a trust, after the grantor has received the repayment of a note given by the trust

for the purchase of assets sold to the trust by the grantor, through the use of a sale to an IDGT.

4. **Gifts of homes and the appreciation in a residence** may be given to designated beneficiaries, after the settlor has used the home for a specific term, through the use of a QPRT.
5. **Charitable gifts** may be used to fulfill philanthropic purposes and to obtain charitable deductions.
6. Gifts to charity may be made in trust, after the settlor has received an annuity or unitrust interest for a specified period, through the use of a **CRT**.
7. Gifts to charity may be made in trust to a charity for a specified period; the balance may then be distributed to designated beneficiaries through the use of a **CLT**.
8. Gifts to charities may be made through a **private foundation** that is managed by a trust or corporation. The foundation may receive its tax exemption, and gifts may be deducted during life and at the time of death.
9. Charitable gifts may be made through trusts or foundations while simultaneously **transferring wealth to family members** through insurance or other vehicles.
10. Estate **gifting plans, creditor protection, and estate organization** may be achieved by the use of a combination of various planning vehicles through the combined uses of ILITs, FLPs, CRTs, IDGTs, CLTs, and private foundations.

CHAPTER FIVE – ESTATE AND FIDUCIARY TAXES

2010 TAX RELIEF ACT

Q & A

Question 1: When did the 2010 Tax Relief Act become **effective**?
Answer: The bill was signed into law on December 17, 2010.

Question 2: When does the 2010 Tax Relief Act expire?
Answer: January 1, 2013.

Question 3: What is the **basic exclusion** amount?
Answer: The amount is $5 million during the term of the act.

Question 4: Do heirs of decedents **dying in 2010** pay an **estate tax or capital gains tax** on the carried-over basis property inherited?
Answer: The 2010 Tax Relief Act gives estates the option of picking either an estate tax or capital gains tax regime.

Question 5: What if a **spouse does not use his or her entire basic exclusion** amount at death?
Answer: The 2010 Tax Relief Act generally grants the surviving spouse the right to transfer or "port" the deceased spouse's unused basic exclusion to his or her own estate. This is referred to a **DSUEA** (deceased spouse's unused exclusion amount).

The 2010 Tax Relief Act was signed into law on December 17, 2010, and extended the 2001 EGTRRA (Economic Growth and

Tax Relief Reconciliation Act) provisions for an additional two years. The 2010 Tax Relief Act **(2010 Act)** made dramatic changes to the gift and estate tax laws, but it was also noteworthy in what it did not change. In particular, it was feared that Congress would correct perceived abuses in the gift and estate transfer system. The 2010 Act did not change or affect (1) the limitations on use of "**discounts**" in family business entities, (2) place limits on or reduce the **GST exemption**, (3) place limitations on the use of "C**rummey withdrawal**" provisions, or (4) set **minimum terms for GRATS**.

The transfer tax provisions in the 2010 Act were contained in Sec. 301-304. The 2010 Act changed the provision for determining the "tentative tax" on gifts, deleting the $1 million exclusion previously in place and replacing it with the applicable exclusion under the act, which is **$5 million**. The act created an "**opt out" rule**, allowing the executors of 2010 decedents to opt out of the estate tax retroactively so that such estates may use the "modified carryover basis" regime that otherwise would apply for decedents dying in 2010 (no estate tax but carryover basis with limited adjustments). The act set forth general time limits for filing estate tax returns, paying taxes, and making disclaimers.

The 2010 Act set the estate tax, gift tax, and GST tax exemptions at $5 million for the duration of the act. The maximum tax rate is set at **35 percent**. Although the GST tax was in effect in 2010, the rate for taxable transfers in 2010 is zero.

The 2010 Act created a new exclusion specifically for married couples referred to as "**portability**." Under this exclusion, a surviving spouse may use any "deceased spouse's unused applicable exclusion amount," i.e., unused $5 million. The deceased spouse's unused exclusion amount is referred to as "**DSUEA**." This is available if the deceased spouse's estate elects to make that unused exclusion amount available. Only the DSUEA of the "last" deceased spouse can be used, and that last spouse's executor must file a timely 706 estate tax return. Once the DSUEA election is made, it is irrevocable. The basic concept is that any exclusion amount not used by the first deceased spouse's estate can be preserved for use by the surviving spouse's estate. This would allow for the simplification of estate planning by **avoiding the need to "split assets"** between the estates of spouses in order to take full advantage of each spouse's applicable credit. In order to take advantage of portability, the first decedent must have died after January 1, 2011. Unfortunately, portability does not apply to the GST tax exemption.

The 2010 Act retains the unlimited **marital deduction** for transfers between spouses who are US citizens. This deduction is granted for outright gifts as well as gifts in trust for the benefit of the surviving spouse. In most instances, the marital deduction is used in trusts which qualify under IRC Sec. 2056 as a "qualified terminal interest property" **(QTIP)** trust for the surviving spouse.

The 2010 Act retained the rules regarding a **noncitizen spouse**. In the event that the surviving spouse is not a US citizen, the transfer to the surviving spouse will not receive a marital deduction unless the transfer is made in trust. In this instance, a "qualified domestic trust" **(QDT)** must be established that requires a **US trustee** to hold the assets and distribute them in accordance with statutory and regulatory requirements contained in IRC Sec. 2056(A). The noncitizen spouse will not be able to transfer the assets outside of the United States, and all taxes will need to be paid at the surviving spouse's death. In addition, if the QDT assets exceed a certain amount, the trustee may be required to post a bond for security against the trust assets.

Generally, **non-US citizens** do not receive the same benefits as US citizens with regard to gift and estate transfers. Non-US citizens receive a gift tax exemption of $136,000 adjusted for inflation and an estate tax exemption of $60,000 adjusted for inflation.

GIFT TAX

Q & A

Question 1: What is the 2011 **gift tax exclusion** amount?
Answer: The annual exclusion amount is $13,000, and the lifetime exclusion amount is $5,000,000.

Question 2: How long does the IRS have to challenge a gift reported on a 709 gift tax return?
Answer: In general, three years.

Based upon the 2010 Act, the gift tax lifetime exemption has increased from $1 million to $5 million. This is in addition to the **$13,000 annual gift tax exemption** (adjusted for inflation). If taxable gifts are made that exceed $13,000 in value, a **709 gift tax return** must be filed; this will set in motion a **three-year statute of limitation** for the return to be challenged. It is important to note that the IRS challenges to gift tax returns focus on the detail of the **gift computation** and all of the background information used to support the value of the gift. In the event that a discounted gift is made, the 709 must substantiate the reasons and conclusions for electing a particular value for the gift.

Because of the great increase in the gift tax lifetime exclusion, many individuals after 2010 have **accelerated the timing and amount of gifts being made** before the expiration of the act in 2013. Nevertheless, the amount of gifting depends upon the individual's net worth and the result the gift will have upon the recipient. Gifts continue to be made outright and through GRATS, sales to IDGTS, Crummey gifting trusts funded with insurance and other assets, and a variety of other transfer methods.

One of the main concerns individuals have when establishing a gifting plan is how the enrichment of the recipient will affect his or her character. As a result of this concern, many gifting trusts have been constructed that **give incentives to the beneficiaries** to accomplish some type of positive behavior before the trustee is required to make any substantial distributions. As long as these incentives are within public policy, they are generally acceptable.

GENERATION-SKIPPING TRANSFER TAX

Q & A

Question 1: What is the **GST tax**?
Answer: The generation-skipping transfer tax is a tax on transfers to "skipped persons," e.g., grandchildren.

Question 2: What **types of transfers** are subject to GST tax?
Answer: The types are generally direct skips, distributions from trusts made to skipped persons, and terminations of trusts to skipped persons.

Question 3: How does an individual **avoid the GST** tax?
Answer: In most cases, a GST exemption is available and may be allocated either automatically or specifically on a 709 form.

Question 4: Can a trust be established that takes advantage of the GST exemption and shelters assets from the GST tax?
Answer: Yes. A legacy or dynasty trust may be established, and assets within the settlor's available GST exemption may be used to fund the trust.

The generation-skipping transfer tax **(GST tax)** is imposed in addition to gift and estate taxes when transfers are made to skipped persons. Generally, most people think of grandchildren as **skipped persons**, but the definition is much more complex than that. In order to understand who a skipped person is, one must first understand who the **transferor** is for GST purposes. This is important in order to apply the transferor's GST exemption against as GST transfer. It is also important to understand what types of transfers are subject to the GST tax.

Generally, the GST tax is imposed against three types of transfers: (1) **direct skips**, (2) **taxable distributions**, and (3) **taxable terminations**. A direct skip can be made outright by a direct transfer of assets, interests, or value to a skipped person. A direct skip can also be made through a disposition via a trust, e.g., a distribution to a grandchild. In the event that a transfer is made in trust and the beneficiaries under the trust who receive distributions are skipped persons, the distribution is subject to GST tax as a taxable distribution. Likewise, if a transfer is made in trust and the trust terminates in favor of skipped persons, the distribution is subject to GST tax as a taxable termination.

Whenever a person creates an estate plan that will result in assets being distributed to persons who are more than one generation below the transferor, a review of the GST tax exemption and applicability must be made. The **GST tax exemption** is only available to a distribution or trust if the term of the trust and the beneficiaries are ascertainable when the trust is created. If the transfer may revert back to the transferor, then the estate tax inclusion period **(ETIP)** will be unascertainable, and the GST tax exemption will not be applicable to the transaction.

Under the 2010 Act, the **GST tax exemption is $5 million** and may be applied to any GST transfer qualifying within the ETIP rules. Each US citizen may allocate his or her GST exemption, resulting in a married couple being able to allocate $10 million of GST exemption if done properly, although there is no portability of the GST tax exemption. In the event that an individual does not allocate his or her GST tax exemption, an automatic allocation will be made for the individual; in some instances, a person may wish to opt out of the automatic GST allocation after analyzing the best use of the exemption.

In the event that a GST taxable transfer is made in trust, the trust, either by its own terms or under state law, must be able to divide trust estates into **GST exempt** shares and **GST non-exempt** shares for ease of allocation, accounting, and taxation. In many instances, shares of trusts that are exempt from GST tax will continue in trust for the lives of the beneficiaries and never be subject to GST tax. In this instance, the trust must not be altered in a manner that would extend the term of the trust and cause the GST exemption to lapse. Likewise, shares of trust that are not exempt from GST tax will generally be distributed to non-skipped persons. It is possible under Missouri law to create a trust that is fully exempt from GST tax that will continue into perpetuity; such a trust is sometimes referred to as a **dynasty or legacy trust**.

706 FEDERAL ESTATE TAX RETURNS

Q & A

Question 1: When is a 706 **estate tax return required** to be filed?
Answer: If an estate is over the basic exclusion amount of $5 million, a 706 must be filed. If a spouse's estate wishes to transfer, i.e., port, that person's unused basic exclusion amount to the second spouse's estate, a 706 must be filed at the time of the death of the first spouse.

Question 2: What must **be revealed** on an individual's estate tax return?
Answer: All worldwide assets must be valued and itemized on an estate tax return.

If a decedent who is a US citizen dies and has worldwide assets **exceeding the $5 million basic exclusion**, a 706 estate tax return is required to be filed by his or her executor or trustee. An estate tax return is similar to other returns in that it requires all the vital information about the decedent that one would expect. On the other hand, an estate tax return is very different from other returns, because it requires the executor to reveal **all of the worldwide assets** owned by the decedent at the time of his or her death. In addition, the **value of all assets must be substantiated** by corresponding evidence, appraisals, or statements rendered by financial institutions or experts. An estate tax return will also need to be filed at the death of the first spouse if the second spouse intends to "port" the unused estate tax exclusion of the first spouse, even if the estate value is less than the basic exclusion amount.

The estate tax return begins by requiring a recapitulation of the **gross (total) estate**. This amount is determined by totaling the decedent's real estate, stocks, bonds, mortgages, notes, cash, insurance on the decedent's life owned by the decedent, jointly owned property, transfers made during the decedent's life in trust or otherwise, powers to appoint property, and annuities.

Next, the estate tax return allows the executor of the estate to take certain **deductions**. Accordingly, deductions are granted for funeral expenses, debts of the decedent, mortgages, liens, losses and expenses incurred during the estate administration, bequests to the surviving spouse, and bequests to charity.

After the gross estate is determined and all deductions have been allocated against the estate, the **tentative taxable estate** is determined. If there is a state death tax, this amount will qualify as an additional deduction. The taxable estate is then determined, taking into account all adjusted taxable gifts made by the decedent. The **tentative tax** is then computed against the adjusted estate. A further adjustment can be made for the total gift tax paid, and the gross estate tax is determined. After the gross estate tax is determined, the applicable credit based upon the remaining basic exclusion, credit for foreign taxes, and credit for prior transfers are subtracted from the gross tax to determine the **net estate tax.** From this amount, GST taxes payable are taken into consideration and the **balance due** is finally computed.

In the event that an estate tax is due, the executor may wait six months after the decedent's death and figure the estate taxes based upon the **alternate valuation** of the estate at that time. **Special**

use valuations for certain types of property may also be taken, if applicable.

The estate tax return must also reveal the **beneficiaries** of the estate and show what proportions each beneficiary will receive of the estate. The return will require the executor to reveal what property, if any, was held in a spousal QTIP trust and if federal **gift tax returns** were ever filed on behalf of the decedent, with copies of the same attached to the return. In addition, the executor will need to reveal if any **property listed** was (1) held as joint property, (2) held as partnership property, (3) subject to valuation discounts, (4) held in trust, (5) held under a GST trust, (6) a closely held entity, (7) subject to a power of appointment, (8) in a financial account in a foreign country, or (9) subject to a trust for which a deduction was claimed by the estate of a predeceased spouse.

Numerous **schedules** will most likely need to be attached to the estate tax return in order to more fully describe the details of all assets listed. These schedules will include details regarding stocks, bonds, mortgages, notes, insurance, jointly held property, miscellaneous property such as jewelry, clothing, and automobiles, transfers made in trust and gift tax payable within three years of the decedent's death, powers to appoint property, expenses that include attorney and accountant fees, bequests to a surviving spouse, and GST transfers. Each schedule will need to substantiate the value of each item listed and explain why any items are not listed at full fair market value. **Appraisals or signed statements of value** will be necessary for most items.

The estate tax return may be **extended for an additional six months** for a total of fifteen months, but, in this event, an **estimated payment** must be made with the extension. Prudence would dictate that the estimated payment be accurate in order to circumvent any penalties or interests on the payment finally due. The estate tax return or the extension must be made in a timely manner not to exceed nine months after the decedent's death (unless death occurred in 2010; special rules then apply).

If the estate tax was miscalculated based upon a good faith error, it is possible to obtain an **estate tax refund** based upon a revised return being filed with substantiating evidence. In the event that the estate tax return is not filed in a timely manner or the information is not accurate, additional taxes may be due, along with heavy **penalties and interests** from the date due. In the event that the estate tax return is **audited** by the IRS, the executor must be ready to supply the examiner with all documentation requested, along with detailed reasons for any adjustments made on the return. Therefore, no adjustments to values should ever be anticipated unless detailed and reasonable calculations were previously made within the safe harbors laid out by the IRS or the tax court. After the IRS and the US Department of Treasury have approved the estate tax return, a closing letter will be given to the executor and the tax preparer stating that no tax remains due unless a further examination is warranted. Absent fraud, the tax return will be final after the **statute of limitations** of three years.

STATE INHERITANCE TAX

Q & A

Question 1: What is the **Missouri inheritance tax**?
Answer: Missouri currently has no estate tax.

Prior to the 2001 Tax Act, most states had their own inheritance tax that was coupled together with the credit for state death tax granted under the IRC. After the 2001 Tax Act, the **state death tax credit** was gradually reduced until it was eliminated entirely in 2005. As a result, many states, which were decoupled from the federal estate tax system, instituted their own standalone inheritance tax. Missouri did not reinstate an independent state inheritance tax after the 2005 elimination of the credit for state death taxes. Nevertheless, many individuals own property in multiple states; this may bring a nexus or contact sufficient to require the filing of a **state inheritance tax return** and the payment of state inheritance tax. In this instance, the amount of exemption will likely vary from state to state, and the amount that may be deducted from the individual's 706 estate tax return must be analyzed.

VALUATION DISCOUNTS

Q & A

Question 1: How do assets receive a **discounted value** for tax purposes?

Answer: Assets that are subject to **restrictions**, e.g., restrictions on sale, transferability, redemption, dividends, or marketability, do not retain the same value as assets that are freely negotiated without similar restrictions.

Question 2: **How much of a discount** do restricted assets receive?
Answer: The amount of the discount depends upon the amount of the restriction and is based upon the usual discount in the community for similar assets.

Question 3: How does an individual **establish a discounted value**?
Answer: A qualified expert in valuation discounts must be retained in order to gain a discount appraisal that will withstand the IRS' scrutiny.

One of the areas in estate planning that is full of opportunities and risks is the area of gift and estate **assets valuations**. For many years, the law has generally allowed **adjustments** to the value of certain assets based upon fundamental principles of accounting, appraisal methods, restrictions attached to particular assets, and both federal and state statutes, case law, and regulations. Various **statutes** allow the value of gifts to be adjusted, depending upon the manner in which the transfer is made. Numerous **legal cases** have established precedents regarding the adjustment to asset values, although each case depends upon its own special facts and circumstances.

Some asset values may be **frozen** if a certain type of transaction is adhered to and arms-length negotiations are entered. For example, if assets are transferred through a properly structured GRAT or sale to an IDGT, the value for gift and estate taxes may be fixed, and gains may be legally transferred to beneficiaries while the transfer taxation of the underlying asset is minimized.

The area receiving the most attention from practitioners, the IRS, and the tax courts is the area of **valuation discounts** obtained through the holding and transfer of assets through corporations, LLCs, and partnerships. The courts have long acknowledged the viability of valuation discounts in the proper circumstances. For example, if a minority shareholder holds stock subject to certain restrictions, that particular block of stock cannot be valued at a value proportionate to the remaining stock without the value being adjusted in consideration of the restrictions. If a minority shareholder, for example, is restrained from (1) **selling** an interest, (2) **liquidating** an interest, (3) **transferring** an interest, (4) exercising **control** over the corporate affairs, or (5) receiving a share of the corporation's **profits**, the shares of the minority shareholder should receive an adjustment to their value to reflect the restrictions. It is commonly known that a willing buyer would not pay face stock value to a willing seller for shares of a corporation that have restrictions attached to them. In this instance, the buyer would require the seller to make an adjustment to the price of the minority shares in order to compensate them for the restrictions attached to the block of stock. Likewise, if a block of stock contained added benefits of control, profits, or transfer, those shares would have an equivalent **premium** associated with them and would be valued higher than shares that did not have the benefits attached to them.

Most of the challenges to valuation discounts and adjustments have occurred in the areas of **partnerships and LLCs created by family members**. These types of entities are primarily created for valid business purposes, namely creditor protection, ease of centralized management, ease of assets transfer, and as a vehicle for joint ventures. Nevertheless, some individuals have pressed the envelope of the safe harbors promulgated by the IRS and tax courts, which has resulted in caution and tension in the estate planning community. Accordingly, a body of case law concerning these types of transactions has arisen, in addition to **IRS audit analysis**.

In the area of FLPs and LLCs, the IRS has developed an audit procedure that challenges transfers made between related parties based upon certain facts and circumstances that are suspect and indicate the presence of a tax scheme or avoidance of taxation without a business purpose. In the event that an entity such as an FLP or LLC is established **close to the time of a decedent's death**, especially if the founder had a terminal illness, all transfers and discounts may be challenged. If the entity was used as a vehicle for **personal use**, especially if **cash withdrawals** were made arbitrarily and disproportionately or used to pay personal taxes, all transfers and discounts may be challenged. If the entity was used to provide **personal loans** to the founding partners, especially if the loans were not documented, all transfers and discounts may be challenged. If the entity was **funded with a majority of the decedent's assets**, especially large blocks of stock with a low cost basis, all transfers and discounts may be challenged. If the entity **did not actively manage** the assets within it, all transfers and discounts may be challenged. If the entity clearly had **no business purpose**, all transfers and discounts may be challenged. If the entity did not maintain a **separate bank account under a separate tax ID number**, all transfers and discounts may be challenged. If the partners of the entity did not make **pro rata contributions** when the entity was established, i.e., only the decedent made contributions, all transfers and discounts may be challenged. If the entity was **formed under a power of attorney**, especially if the **documents were not in order**, all transfers and discounts may be challenged. If the entity's income was not distributed pro rata according to the proportionate interest of the partners, all transfers and discounts may be challenged. If the entity's assets and the decedent's **assets were commingled**, all transfers and discounts may be challenged. If the assets funding an entity were **not properly valued or appraised**, all transfers and discounts may be challenged. If an entity was formed and subsequently **dissolved close to the time of the decedent's death**, all transfers and discounts may be challenged. If the **entity was not funded** at the time of the decedent's death, especially if deeds were not prepared or recorded and general partnership interests were not funded, then all transfers and discounts may be challenged. If the entity did not keep up **customary business procedures**, all transfers and discounts may be challenged. If the entity was not managed by the general partner or managing member but by someone else, all transfers and discounts may be challenged. If the entity's assets remained in **money markets and fixed investments** without diversification from the time of creation until the decedent's death, all transfers and discounts may be challenged. Finally, if the entity's assets were never managed and **distributions were never made**, all transfers and discounts may be challenged.

When dealing with valuation discounts, the first review should be based upon the entity's internal agreement or operating agreement. **State statutes** will grant certain restrictions and will allow certain restrictions to be placed in the **governing document**. If the restrictions comport with the state requirements and are set forth in the governing document, the restriction will generally be upheld, and a **reasonable adjustment** to the unit vale will be allowed. The amount of the valuation discount will need to be made by an expert who reduced his or her opinion into a **discount appraisal report**.

The basic challenge made against transfers receiving valuation discounts is based upon the presumption that the transfer was a device to transfer an interest to the object of the decedent's bounty for **less than full and adequate consideration** through money or some other interest having value. All transfers through an entity must be in accordance with a "**bona fide business arrangement**." Accordingly, the establishment of an entity between related parties and the transfer of interests between the parties must not be deemed to have been established primarily for estate planning, tax reduction, wealth transfer, or the tax free disposition among family members.

In order to avoid IRS challenges, the entity must be established for a bona fide business reason and **not be a step transaction** to avoid taxation. After the entity is established, **transfers may be made in normal and customary periods**, depending upon the nature of the assets. When an entity is formed, all family members who are entering into the joint venture should make pro rata contributions. The business purpose of the entity must be for a **legitimate and nontax reason**. The decedent, i.e., founder of the entity, must retain sufficient assets outside of the entity to live, and there should **be no commingling** of personal and entity assets. The founder/decedent should **not maintain control** of the entity and should not receive a disproportionate amount of the entity's income or assets. In order to qualify gifts of entity units as excluded annual gifts, it may be necessary to grant partners and members the current right to withdraw entity assets via "Crummey withdrawal rights" in order to give all of the partners the immediate use, possession, and **enjoyment of their interests**.

All valuation adjustments should be made with the assistance of a qualified valuation appraiser. All valuation discounts should be made within the accepted parameters indicated by the IRS and the tax courts.

1041 FIDUCIARY INCOME TAX RETURNS

Q & A

Question 1: When does a trust need to file its own **1041 tax return**?
Answer: Usually when a trust becomes irrevocable, e.g., after the death of a settlor or upon the establishment of an irrevocable trust.

Question 2: What **tax identification number** is used on a 1041 fiduciary return?
Answer: Generally, a living trust may no longer use the settlor's social security number and report taxes under the settlor's 1040 after the settlor's death. The trust must obtain a new tax identification number for reporting income on the 1041.

Before a trustee files an income tax return, it is first necessary to review the taxable status of the trust. If the trust is a **grantor trust**, e.g., a revocable trust, all of the trust income is distributed through the trust to the settlor who reports the income on his or her individual 1040. In this instance, a separate tax return and separate tax ID number is not necessary. If the trust has become irrevocable, e.g., at the incapacity or death of the settlor, a separate tax ID number and a separate fiduciary tax return must be filed by the successor trustee.

Subchapter J of the IRC contains the rules and regulations concerning the income taxation of trusts. Under state law, the trustee of a trust holds the legal title to trust property, and so the trustee is taxable on all income received by the trust. The requirement to distribute income will be dictated by the terms and conditions of the trust.

All trust income is reported by the trustee on a **1041 fiduciary income tax return.** The trustee also deducts all expenses against income on the return. The net income remaining after deduction of expenses becomes the basis for calculating distributable net income referred to as "**DNI**." DNI does two things: (1) it measures the amount of taxable income that is distributed from the trustee to the beneficiaries for purposes of shifting income to the beneficiaries, and (2) it insures that the income distributed by the trustee to the beneficiaries will have the same substantive tax to the beneficiaries as the trustee would have had.

The trustee receives an income tax deduction for distributions to beneficiaries. The income that a trustee is required to distribute is referred to as fiduciary accounting income **(FAI)**. If the trustee is not required to make distributions, the income received by the trust must be reported and taxes paid at compressed rates; e.g., 2011 rates reach the top marginal bracket after $11,300 of trust income. In the event that the trust pays out its income, then the beneficiaries pick up the income via a K-1 and pay income tax in their respective tax brackets.

Trusts must be categorized under Subchapter J as being either simple or complex. This is required in order to determine the personal exemptions allowed to the trust and to calculate the distribution deduction available to the fiduciary. To be classified as a **simple trust**, a trust must (1) be required under the governing instrument to **distribute all income** currently for the taxable year, and (2) the governing instrument may not provide for any amounts to be paid, permanently set aside, or used for **charitable purposes** during the taxable year. A simple trust determines its distribution deduction on the basis of what was required to be paid out to beneficiaries, not what was actually paid.

Although a trust may be considered a single trust under state and federal law, if the trust has more than one beneficiary and different beneficiaries have substantially separate and independent shares, their shares are treated as separate trusts for purposes of determining DNI. In this way, each beneficiary's share is treated separately for tax purposes. Accordingly, a residuary trust, marital trust, or trusts for children or grandchildren may be treated as **separate shares for tax purposes**.

IRC Sec. 663(b) allows the trustees to elect to treat any amount or portion thereof that is properly paid or credited to a beneficiary within the **65 days** following the close of a taxable year as an amount that was properly paid or credited on the last day of that taxable year. This allows a trust some latitude in making distributions at the end of each taxable year. The paying of gifts, bequests, and distributions and reporting them as fiduciary accounting income or distributable net income must be carefully determined by a CPA or other qualified tax consultant. The preparation of a 1041 is a complicated matter that is very different from an individual's 1040 tax return. Nevertheless, a 1041 must be prepared for each taxable year in which a simple or complex trust holds assets and makes income.

Top 10 Planning Tips

1. Review all estate plans with consideration of the **basic exclusion amount** of $5 million.
2. Review the use of **portability** of the basic exclusion amount between spouses.
3. Review the implication of transfers to **noncitizen spouses** and the use of a qualified domestic trust.
4. Review gifting in consideration of the **lifetime gift tax exclusion** of $5 million.
5. Review transfers to lower generations in consideration of **the generation transfers tax exclusion** of $5 million.
6. Consider the filing of a 706 **estate tax return** to use a deceased spouse's unused exclusion amount.
7. Review estate plans with consideration of Missouri having repealed its **state inheritance tax** while considering any other state that may impose a separate inheritance tax.
8. Consider the use of **valuation discounts** that the law and the IRS may allow. Also review the use of partnerships, corporations, limited liability companies, and other trusts that would allow the transfer of assets with adjusted values for tax purposes.
9. Review the need to file 1041 **fiduciary tax returns** regarding irrevocable trusts and other entities that do not qualify for "grantor trust" status.
10. Review all estate plans in light of the scheduled **sunset of the 2010 Tax Relief Act in 2013**.

CHAPTER SIX – CONCLUSIONS

PUTTING IT ALL TOGETHER

Q & A

Question 1: What type of an estate plan should a husband and wife with children and a **small estate** have?
Answer: At the very least, an individual or a couple just starting out should have a will naming guardians. Additionally, each person should have a durable power of attorney allowing each party to transact business on behalf of the other. Lastly, each person should have a health care directive allowing the other party to make medical decisions on behalf of the other person in the event of a medical emergency.

Question 2: What type of an estate plan should an individual or a husband and wife with a **mid-sized estate** have?
Answer: The basic estate planning instruments such as a will, durable power of attorney, and health care directives should always be used. In addition, the parties should consider the use of a revocable living trust, especially if a relatively large amount of life insurance has been procured against either party's life. A trust will ensure that the estate will be left for the benefit of spouse and children in an orderly manner and without probate.

Question 3: What type of estate plan should an individual or husband and wife with a **large estate** have?

Answer: The basic estate planning instruments such as a will, durable power of attorney, and health care directive should always be used. In addition, individual revocable living trusts should be considered in order to not only avoid probate, but also to plan for taxes. Coordination of assets and detailed reviews of beneficiary designations must be made. The dispositive plan of distribution must be analyzed carefully, and the effects of the inheritance must be considered.

Question 4: What type of estate plan should a **wealthy** individual or husband and wife have?
Answer: The basic estate planning instruments such as a will, durable power of attorney, health care directives, and revocable living trusts should always be used. In addition, the leveraging of estate tax payments should be reviewed. The systematic transfer of wealth through basic and sophisticated gifting techniques should be considered. Lastly, charitable transfers in trust or otherwise should be reviewed. The parties' mission for the entrustment of wealth should be carefully reviewed and implemented over time.

After reviewing the materials in this booklet, a question arises: Is there a **simple yet comprehensive** way to cover a person's estate plan? The answer is yes. However, the basics of estate planning must be understood by those who are setting out to develop a plan. Once the rudimentary **concepts** have been understood, a **design** can be developed that addresses the desires and needs of the individual.

Organization of a person's assets is the beginning of an estate plan and is followed by a time of deep decision making concerning who will manage the estate and who will receive its benefits. Once the proper **estate documents** have been decided upon and have been integrated with one another, the retitling of assets can be made in a manner consistent with those documents. As a result, the **probability of financial success** will increase exponentially.

As a basic plan, each person should have a will, power of attorney, and health care directive. The **power of attorney** will allow someone to act for the individual in the event of an emergency. The **health care directive** will also allow someone to make medical decisions in emergency situations, especially if an individual becomes incapacitated. In the event that death occurs, a **last will and**

testament gives direction as to who shall receive the individual's assets and who will assist with the administration of those assets.

In order to avoid the probate process, the Non-Probate Transfer Act should be used, and **POD and TOD designations** should be placed upon as many assets as is necessary. For example, automobiles and real estate should have beneficiary designations on their titles that will allow for automatic transfer at the owner's death.

As an individual's estate value grows and the complexity of distribution increases, the use of **a revocable living trust**, along with a power of attorney, pour-over will, and health care directive, will become appropriate. As a general premise, an estate with a value of over $500,000 may use a revocable living trust to avoid probate and to make detailed distributions to beneficiaries.

Estates containing relatively large retirement assets, insurance, and sophisticated investments will require detailed reviews of **beneficiary designations** in light of current tax laws. As estate values increase, the use of irrevocable **insurance trusts, partnerships, and limited liability companies** may be necessary to manage the estate.

In the event that an estate is large enough for the individual owners to feel that they do not need their entire estate in order to sustain their lifestyle, gifting assets to family, loved ones, and charities is an option that should be reviewed. In this instance, the use of **charitable trusts, grantor retained trusts, and intentionally defective trusts** may be used to accomplish the individual's goals.

Each person's estate assets and desired plan must be reviewed in order to find the right mix of planning options. An **estate planning attorney** must be used in order to understand the many details contained in the formation of a plan and the **correct drafting** of the underlying documentation. Estate planning, like so many other specialties in life, cannot be done by the layperson without a high probability of serious mistakes being made. After a fundamental estate plan has been developed and implemented, the plan and documents must be **periodically reviewed** in order to stay abreast of current legal changes and changes in a person's life. Once this has been done, a person can maintain his or her estate with the satisfaction of being a good steward. An individual who is prepared can have peace of mind and know that he or she has **properly cared for** family and loved ones.

Top 10 Planning Tips

1. **Guardians** should always be nominated under an individual's last will and testament.
2. **Avoiding probate** through the use of trust or non-probate transfers should always be considered.
3. Provisions for the use of **backup agents** and attorneys-in-fact should always be made through the use of health care directives and durable powers of attorney.
4. **Estate management** should be accomplished within revocable living trusts, limited liability companies, partnerships, or other entities in order to provide organization, creditor protection, and orderly disposition.
5. Individuals should make **detailed plans for the management and disposition** of their estates, especially concerning incentives and controls for the use of wealth for future generations.
6. **Tax planning** must be addressed in large estates. A detailed review of the income taxation of retirement accounts and other matters concerning IRD must be made. A detailed review of the gifting options available should be made in order to accommodate the orderly transfer of wealth. A detailed analysis of estate tax projections must be made in order to properly plan for the payment of these taxes.
7. Consideration of **charitable and philanthropic objectives** must be made in order to properly implement them into an estate plan.
8. Giving **lifetime gifts** to loved ones should be considered in order to financially assist children and friends.
9. The **transfer of wealth** must be considered under a number of circumstances. Tax results must be carefully reviewed, in addition to the specific types of assets to be transferred. The impact of wealth being granted to individuals must be considered. The use of complex estate planning techniques and sophisticated documents must be carefully evaluated.
10. The **ultimate purpose** of estate transfer must be determined so the individual can be satisfied that the estate is in order and will continue to be transferred in accordance with his or her wishes and desires.

Mr. Michael Magliari graduated Magna Cum Laude from Missouri Baptist College in 1978 and from the Saint Louis University School of Law in 1983. From 1986 to 1996, he was a partner with the law firm of Briegel, Baylard, PC, serving as managing partner from 1992 through 1995. In 1998, Mr. Magliari founded Michael E. Magliari, P.C.

Mr. Magliari has been a frequent lecturer and estate planning counsel for numerous charitable organizations, insurance companies, investment firms, and trust companies throughout St. Louis and the surrounding areas.

Mr. Magliari is the chairman of the Probate and Trust Division, Estate Planning and Probate Committee, and Trust Revision Subcommittee of the Missouri Bar Association and a former member of the Ethics Committee of the Bar Association of Metropolitan St. Louis. Mr. Magliari has authored the chapter on trust administration for the Missouri Bar Desktop Series.

Estate Planning: The Fundamental Concepts Under Missouri Law

SUPPLEMENTAL MATERIAL 2013-2016

CHAPTER TWO – HEALTHCARE DIRECTIVES AND POWERS OF ATTORNEY

RIGHT OF SEPULCHER

In order to clarify the order of the individual(s) authorized to control and choose a person's funeral and final resting place, Missouri has enacted RSMo. Section 194.119. This authority is referred to as the "right of sepulcher," and a person has the right to appoint the individual to act in this capacity. If a person has not exercised this right, the statute allows the "next-of-kin" to make these decisions, and provides a list for the individuals that qualify as "next-of-kin" for this purpose (e.g., Attorney-in-fact under a Durable Power of Attorney, spouse, and so on). It is particularly important to exercise this right if a person anticipates disagreement within the family regarding his or her final resting place (e.g., if one child wants mother to be buried, but the other child wants the mother to be cremated, the mother should select the child who agrees with her wishes), or if a person desires a non-family member to make such decisions. This right is likely to be exercised as a component of either a medical directive or a durable power of attorney, or as a wholly separate document.

CHAPTER THREE – ESTATE TRANSFERS IN GENERAL

QUALIFIED SPOUSAL JOINT TRUSTS (QSJT)

Q & A

Question 7: What is **tenancy by the entirety** (TBE) property?
Answer: Property held as husband and wife as joint tenants with the right of survivorship. This is a unique status and form of owning property that is specifically sanctioned by state law.

Question 8: How is **TBE property distinguished** from other forms of ownership?
Answer: It is limited to property held together by a husband and wife and automatically grants protection from the individual creditor of either the husband or wife from attaching TBE property to collect a judgment.

Question 9: Why is a **Qualified Spousal Trust** (QST or QSJT) a beneficial estate planning tool?
Answer: It affords a married couple the opportunity to hold their properties in trust with the TBE creditor protection while taking advantage of the creation of

sub-trusts for both tax planning and distributions of inheritance.

Tenancy by the Entirety in Missouri

The uniqueness of tenancy by the entireties ownership is rooted in the concept that a husband and wife take and hold property **as one person**, each holding the whole of it rather than as separate individuals.

Because the common law viewed tenancy by the entireties property as being owned by one person, neither spouse could dispose of any part of the property held in that tenancy without the consent of the other.

Merrill Lynch v. Shackelford (Mo.App. W.D. 1979) states that the **presumption** that property is held as tenancy by the entireties does not depend on how title to the property is taken as long as the parties are married. It does not matter whether the word "or" was used instead of "and" or if the couple was not referred to as husband and wife. The presumption of tenancy by the entirety is rebuttable.

In Missouri, property held as tenants by the entirety is **not subject to the claims of the creditors of one spouse**; whether property is held by a couple as tenants by the entirety is dependent on a couple's intent; property held by a husband and wife is presumed to be held as tenants by the entirety unless otherwise stipulated; one spouse acting unilaterally cannot sever the tenancy; and, once established, a couple must jointly manifest a clear intent to sever the tenancy.

Tenancy by the Entireties and Trusts under Missouri Case Law

Bolton Roofing Co., Inc. v. Hedrick (Mo.App. S.D. 1985) can be and has been construed to mean that tenancy by the entirety property transferred to a trust (at least a joint trust) **retains its characteristics** as tenancy by the entirety property.

The *Bellingroehr* (Bankr. W.D. Mo 2009) case states that one of the original purposes of the judicial creation of tenancy by the entirety under Missouri law was to protect the wife from the husband who might irresponsibly lose the family home or other assets. "As a result, the primary characteristic of tenancy by the entirety property is that **neither spouse may revoke, terminate, or burden the property unilaterally**" (*Bellingroehr*). "Because the trust in this case possesses the essential restrictions against severability and transferability as entirety property possesses, I find that the Bellingroehrs did not sever the tenancy by transferring the entirety property into the Trust" (*Bellingroehr*).

To be exempt as tenancy by the entirety property, the essential characteristics of tenancy by the entirety must be preserved when that property is transferred to a trust (*Bellingroehr*).

Tenancy by the Entirety, Estate Planning, and Trusts

The trust instrument may provide that any tenancy by the entireties property or other joint property contribution to the trust is automatically split into undivided interests and any property owned by one spouse contributed to the trust would be deemed a gift of an undivided interest to the other spouse.

Missouri Qualified Spousal Joint Trust Statute: R.S.Mo. Section 456.950

To be a QSJT, a joint trust must be **established by spouses**. That trust must establish:

1. A "true" joint trust with assets held for the **benefit of both spouses** as well as discretionary distributees and which is amendable and revocable by either spouse (or both acting together if preferred);

2. A "tax planning" joint trust in which **two or more independent shares** of the trust are created with one share held for the benefit of each spouse with that spouse having the power to revoke or amend the provisions of his or her respective share; or

3. A joint trust that contains **both** the "true" and "tax planning" joint trusts within one trust document.

If a QSJT is established and any property of a spouse is transferred to that QSJT, that property (and all proceeds from any sale of the property and all income from that property) continues to be sheltered from creditor claims against one of the spouses. Additionally, if the trust was created as two separate shares, with each spouse alone having the right to amend or revoke that share and each spouse having a beneficial interest in that spouse's share, then upon the death of the first spouse, that spouse's share can be distributed to a spendthrift trust for the benefit of the survivor. Because the property thereafter held for the benefit of the survivor in the spendthrift trust was clearly the property of the deceased spouse, the spendthrift trust for the benefit of the survivor should not be considered self-settled.

The QSJT statute, as modified and effective on August 28, 2015, applies to any trust before, on, or after that date.

Estate Planning Using QSJTs

It is not unusual for accounts held at financial institutions, particularly brokerage houses, to specifically **not be held as tenancy by the entirety**. Nevertheless, the statute provides that any property held by either or both spouse(s) may be transferred into a QST.

If the QSJT is a **separate share** tax planning trust, a spouse's separate property may be transferred to that spouse's separate share. An option is to keep the spouse's separate property outside of the trust but subject the property to a transfer-on-death designation to the trust at the time of the death of that spouse. This is especially important for a tax planning joint trust because one may not want to have the separate property of the first spouse to die to be subject to provisions of the trust dividing the assets between the two spouses' shares. This is also true for other assets passing to the trust under a beneficiary designation, such as life insurance.

The first amendment to the Qualified Spousal Trust statute created a presumption that any property owned by a husband and wife would be deemed tenants by the entireties property when transferred into a QSJT.

The second amendment also allowed a husband and wife to transfer any of their joint property directly into a QST as tenants by the entirety without the necessity of first designating the property as tenants by the entirety and then subsequently transferring the interest into the trust. Any property or interests in property held as husband and wife, whether as tenants by the entirety or as joint tenants or other form of joint ownership with right of survivorship, is conclusively deemed to be held as tenants by entirety property and may be transferred directly into a QST and thereby obtain creditor protection as tenants by entirety property.

The third amendment to the Qualified Spousal Trust statute became effective on August 28, 2015, and clarifies that a QST applies to all "**spouses**" who create the trust together. This change addressed the concerns promulgated in the US Supreme Court case of *U.S. v. Windsor* (133 S.Ct. 2675 [2013]) by removing the reference to "husband and wife".

The language concerning revocation of a QST was corrected to state that either or both settlors may revoke the trust. This allows the surviving settlor to alter the trust terms or revoke the trust if unanticipated events occur. Notwithstanding the same, joint revocation while both settlors are living is presumed to be necessary to preserve the tenants by entirety property.

The amended statute allows for **discretionary distributions** to persons other than the settlors clarifying that exclusive use of TBE property by the settlors is not required. For example, distributions may be made to the children of the settlors during the settlors' lives.

The amended statute also provides for property to be transferred into a QST **without regard to how it was titled prior** to it being held in the trust. This allows for individual spouses to separately transfer property into a QST as they could to any other tenants by the entirety account. This amendment allows for spouses with individual trusts to transfer those assets directly into a qualified spousal trust and obtain tenancy by the entirety protection.

The amended statute also provides for property in the trust to receive the same treatment for **bankruptcy purposes** as tenancy by the entirety property would receive as a matter of state law.

The amended statute also clarifies that property contributed to a qualified spousal trust will **not be affected by a dissolution of marriage** unless expressly agreed upon in writing. Accordingly, if a spouse desires to transfer separate property into a QST, the best practice would suggest the use of a postnuptial agreement to clarify the property's disposition pursuant to divorce.

The amended statute also clearly states no transfers to a qualified spousal trust may defeat the **Missouri Uniform Fraudulent Transfers Act**. Thus, any transfer made by a settlor during a period when the settlor knew or should have known the transfer would defeat, hinder, or delay a creditor's ability to enforce a judgment or cause of action at the time of the transfer will have no effect and can be set aside by a court.

In addition, companion statute **R.S.Mo. Section 456.1-113** clarifies any transfer of assets to a qualified spousal trust or any other trust may be **made or titled to the trustee**

of the trust or to the trust itself. Such a transfer may be made to and titled in a specific share of the trust without the share being partitioned or converted into property held as tenants in common. This allows an asset to be titled in the name of a trustee, in the name of a trust, or in the name of a share of a trust.

Drafting for QSJTs

Each **separate share** of the surviving spouse may be revocable by one settlor without the participation or consent of the other settlor after the first spouse's death. Subsequent to the *Brewer* case in the United States Bankruptcy Court (544 B.R. 177 [2015]), the most conservative approach would be to draft the trust instrument requiring both spouses to revoke all shares.

If the settlors intend that the separate property of one settlor go to that settlor's separate share, that intent should be clearly stated in both the Qualified Spousal Trust and in the account titles and/or beneficiary designations for assets going to the separate share. This could be accomplished by designating different shares within the trust agreement and titling specific property into specific shares, e.g., husband's share, wife's share, joint share, or proportional shares.

If **separate property** is contributed to a Qualified Spousal Trust, it may become **commingled** with assets that were originally held in tenancy by the entirety for purposes of establishing marital property. It may be simpler, and is certainly safer for divorce purposes, to only transfer property held by spouses together to the tax planning Qualified Spousal Trust and keep all separate property titled in the respective spouse's separate name subject to a transfer-on-death (TOD) designation to the trust. Nevertheless, separate property can be transferred to a Qualified Spousal Trust and made subject to a **postnuptial agreement**.

TRUST DECANTING

Q & A

Question 1: What is **trust decanting**?
Answer: Trust decanting is the ability of a trustee of a discretionary trust to transfer the assets of such existing discretionary trust to a new trust referred to as a second trust.

Question 2: **Why** would a trustee use decanting?
Answer: If a trust's terms were no longer beneficial to the beneficiaries or no longer harmonized with the tax law or facts and circumstances surrounding the trust administration, the trustee may change the terms of the trust in order to correct an evolving deficiency.

Question 3: May a trustee decant without giving **notice** of their intent to do so?
Answer: No. The decanting trustee must give notice to the beneficiaries of the second trust. Based on the trustee's discretion to distribute, only the beneficiaries of the second trust are required to receive notice.

Question 4: Are there **limitations** to the trustee's ability to decant?
Answer: Yes. The statute imposes technical and practical limitations on decanting in order to preserve the integrity of the original trust for both tax purposes and to maintain the settlor's purposes. Furthermore, the decanting trustee

should always carefully consider the income, estate, and GST tax ramifications of creating a second trust.

Question 5: **What property** may be decanted?
Answer: Any property held in trust where the trustee has discretion over the payment of income or principal. The Missouri statute specifically prohibits decanting in certain circumstances, so a review of the statute is necessary in each case.

Introduction

A decanting power allows modifications to a discretionary trust via the creation of a new trust altogether.

Decanting can be used for improving administrative efficiency; responding to changing statutory or case law; correcting scrivener's errors; dividing the trust; merging smaller trusts; forming and distributing to a supplemental needs trust; postponing otherwise mandatory distributions; allowing the removal or appointment of trustees; changing provisions for trustee compensation; changing the trust situs; adding a spendthrift clause; and other changed circumstances (facilitating any number of other tax or other kinds of planning strategies).

The trustee of a Missouri discretionary trust possesses this power by default. However, if the trust expressly prohibits decanting, a trustee may not exercise it.

A trustee may decant a trust regardless of its age as long as either the income or principal distributions are discretionary under the terms and conditions of the trust instrument.

The Decanting Statute: R.S.Mo. Section 456.4-419

Missouri allows the decanting of a trust if *either* the trust income or the principal is subject to discretionary distribution.

The presence of **ascertainable standards** (e.g., health, education, maintenance, and support) is irrelevant to the general authority to decant. Therefore, a trustee may decant a trust when distributions are subject to limitations set forth within it.

Decanting does not need to be of the entire trust property. **Partial interests** of the trust or **separate shares** may be decanted.

The second trust does not need to have been created by the terms of the first trust agreement but can be newly created. Note also that this language does not require that the decanted assets (in the second trust) be held for the same beneficiaries as the first trust.

Before decanting, the trustee is required first to "take into account" **three distinct factors**: the terms and purposes of the first trust, the terms and purposes of the second trust, and the consequences of the distribution. If these factors have been met, the trustee is free to decant.

The **notice** provision of the statute requires the trustee to provide beneficiaries (*only* of the second trust) 60 days' notice of the decanting, although a beneficiary may waive that right. If there will be current beneficiaries of the intended second trust, the trustee must notify them (and only them), but if not, the trustee must notify the "qualified beneficiaries" (typically the remaindermen) of the second trust.

A decanting trustee is bound by all of the **fiduciary duties** imposed by common law and by the trust agreement at hand. This provision makes explicit that the mere presence of the decanting statute does not create a duty for the trustee to decant or even to consider decanting.

A trustee may decant to a trust that includes any of the same "current or contingent" **beneficiaries**. It is possible for a trustee to decant to a new trust for the current benefit of one beneficiary who had previously been a contingent remainder beneficiary. Most strikingly, while a trustee cannot introduce new beneficiaries in the second trust, the trustee can, in effect, abandon beneficiaries of the first trust.

Subdivision (3) of the statute is intended in large measure to prevent a decanting trustee from unknowingly creating a tax liability.

The statute does impose **limitations** on the trustee's ability to decant. For example, a trustee who is also a beneficiary generally cannot decant unless the trustee's distributive power is limited by an ascertainable standard. When decanting, the new trust must contain the same "restrictions" on discretionary distributions as were contained in the first trust unless a distribution is "needed" for a distribution to a beneficiary under an ascertainable standard. The second trust agreement must require a minor beneficiary's interest to vest no later than it would have under the terms of the first trust. A trustee cannot decant property subject to a *Crummey* power unless the decanting does not alter that power. Even more succinctly, a trustee can only decant if decanting does not change the *Crummey* power.

Tax Considerations

The general rule is that a trust is "grandfathered" out of **generation-skipping tax (GST)** if it was irrevocable on or before September 25, 1985. Final regulations were issued in December 2000 and include four "safe harbor" modifications to GST trusts: the exercise of discretionary trustee powers, court-approved settlements, judicial-construction orders, and modifications that do not "shift a beneficial interest in the trust to any beneficiary who occupies a lower generation." Accordingly, a trustee who is decanting must carefully take into consideration the GST status and impact of the act of decanting prior to proceeding to avoid any negative consequences to the GST trust.

TRUST PROTECTORS

Q & A

Question 1: What is a **trust protector** (TP)?
A TP is an individual who is granted powers under a trust document to make specific adjustments to the trust in order to solve problems that may arise. These powers may be used presently or in the future after the trust has become irrevocable.

Question 2: What is the **scope** of the TP's authority?
Answer: The trust document grants the powers given to the TP unless the Missouri statute specifically prohibits specific powers from being exercised.

Question 3: How is a trust protector granted **powers**?
Answer: A trust protector is granted powers under a trust instrument. The specific powers granted to the trust protector will limit his or her ability to affect the trust estate.

Question 4: Are there **limitations** to a trust protector's powers?
Answer: Yes. A trust protector is restricted from certain actions set forth in the statute. For example, a trust protector may not be granted power that would circumvent a marital or charitable deduction previously applicable to a trust estate. In addition, the trust document may also set forth limitations.

Question 5: Does a trust protector act as a **fiduciary**?
Answer: A trust protector must act in a "fiduciary capacity" in carrying out the powers granted. However, a trust protector is not a trustee and will not be held to a trustee's fiduciary standard unless he or she is carrying out the duties of a trustee.

Question 6: Is a trust protector ever **exonerated** from liability?
Answer: Yes. A trust protector is exonerated from liability unless it is proven that he or she acted in bad faith or with reckless indifference.

Powers to Direct – Appointment of Trust Protector, Powers, Limitations

A trust instrument may provide for the appointment of a trust protector. A trust protector appointed in the trust instrument shall have only the powers granted to the trust protector by the express terms of the trust instrument.

Express powers that may be granted include, but are not limited to, the following: remove and appoint a trustee; modify or amend the trust instrument to achieve favorable tax status, reflect legal changes that affect trust administration, correct errors or ambiguities, or correct a drafting error; increase, decrease, modify, or restrict the interests of the beneficiaries; terminate the trust; change the applicable law; or such other powers as are expressly granted.

The statute provides that a **trust protector shall have no power to** modify a trust to: remove a requirement from a trust created to meet the requirements of 42 U.S.C. Section 1396(d)(4) to pay back a governmental entity for benefits; or reduce or eliminate an income interest of the income beneficiary of any of the following types of trusts: a trust for which a marital deduction has been taken; a charitable remainder trust; a grantor retained annuity trust; or a trust for which an election as a qualified Sub-Chapter S Trust under Section 1361(d) of the Internal Revenue Code is currently in place.

Except to the extent otherwise specifically provided in a trust instrument, the trust protector shall not exercise a power in a way that would result in a taxable gift.

Except to the extent otherwise provided in the trust instrument and in the statute, and notwithstanding any provision of R.S.Mo. Sections 456.1-101 to 456.11-1106 to the contrary, a trust protector shall **act in a fiduciary capacity** in carrying out the powers granted to the trust protector in the trust instrument and shall have such duties to the beneficiaries, the settlor, or the trust as set forth in the trust instrument. A trust protector is **not a trustee**. A trust protector is not liable for the acts or omissions of any fiduciary or beneficiary under the trust instrument. A trust protector is exonerated from any and all liability for the trust protector's acts or omissions, or arising from any exercise or nonexercise of the powers expressly conferred on the trust protector in the trust instrument, unless it is established by a preponderance of the evidence that the acts or omissions of the trust protector were done or omitted in breach of the trust protector's duty, **in bad faith, or with reckless indifference**.

A trust protector is authorized to exercise the express powers granted in the trust instrument at any time and from time to time after the trust protector acquires knowledge of their appointment as trust protector and of the powers granted. A trust protector is entitled to receive reasonable **compensation**. A trust protector is entitled to receive reimbursement of the reasonable costs of defending any claim unless it is established by clear and convincing evidence that the trust protector was acting in bad faith or with reckless indifference.

The express powers granted in the trust instrument shall not be exercised by the trust protector for the trust protector's own personal benefit. However, examples of **powers routinely granted** to a trust protector include the power to remove trustees (including an investment advisor or trust advisor); modify or amend the trust; achieve favorable tax status; reflect legal changes; correct errors or ambiguities; correct a drafting error; change the applicable law; modify a trust to qualify as a grantor trust or become disqualified as a grantor trust; consent to a trustee's action or inaction; veto or direct all of part of any trust distribution; increase or decrease any interest; modify a trust to qualify as a supplemental needs trust; authorize distributions to a beneficiary or legal guardian or custodian or supplemental needs trust; or appoint a successor trust protector.

If a trust protector is granted a power in the trust instrument to direct, consent to, or disapprove a trustee's actual or proposed investment decision, distribution decision, or other decision of the trustee required to be performed under applicable trust law in carrying out the duties of the trustee in administering the trust, then only with respect to such power, the **trust protector shall have the same duties and liabilities as if serving as a trustee**. A trustee shall carry out the written directions given to the trustee by a trust protector. The trustee shall have no duty to monitor the conduct of the trust protector.

The trust protector shall be entitled to **receive information** regarding the administration of the trust as follows: upon request of the trust protector; the request of the trust protector for information under this section shall be with respect to a single trust that is sufficiently identified to enable the trustee to locate the records of the trust; and if the trustee is bound by any **confidentiality** restrictions with respect to an asset of a trust, a trust protector who requests information under this section about such asset shall agree to be bound by the confidentiality restrictions that bind the trustee before receiving such information from the trustee.

A trust protector may **resign** by giving 30 days' written notice. A trust protector of a trust having its principal place of administration in this state submits personally to the jurisdiction of the courts.

GIFTING AND ANNUAL GIFT TAX EXCLUSIONS

Q & A

Question 1: What is the **annual gift tax exclusion** amount for 2016?
Answer: The annual gift tax exclusion amount for 2016 is $14,000. As in the past, this amount will be adjusted for inflation in the future.

Question 2: What is the annual gift exclusion amount for a **non-citizen spouse** for the calendar year of 2016?
Answer: The annual exclusion amount for a non-citizen spouse for 2016 is $148,000.

CHAPTER FOUR – ADVANCED PLANNING TECHNIQUES

FAMILY LIMITED PARTNERSHIPS AND VALUATION DISCOUNTS

The tax court has recently focused on the current safe harbors and potential abuses when using a Family Limited Partnership (FLP) in estate planning. For example, in the **Estate of Purdue v. Commissioner**, TC Memo 2015-249, the case dealt with the following three questions:

> Whether the value of assets transferred to an FLP were **includible** in the decedent's gross estate under IRC Sections 2036(a) and 2035(a);
>
> Whether gifts of FLP interests were **gifts** of present interests under IRC Section 2503(b) for gift tax annual exclusion purposes; and

Whether the accrued interest on **loans** made by members of the FLP to the estate to pay the estate tax were **deductible** under IRC Section 2053.

As a matter of best practice, to provide written justification of the business purpose of the entity, a family limited partnership agreement or LLC operating agreement should include the following purposes:

1. Consolidate **management** of the assets;
2. Avoid **fractionalization** of ownership;
3. Retain **ownership** of the assets within the family;
4. Provide **creditor protection**;
5. Provide **flexibility** of management not available through other entities; and

Educate family members and promote communication regarding financial matters.

A court typically analyzes whether the estate and business structure passes the **bona fide sale test** and **adequate and full consideration was given** when a business entity is formed, funded, and interests given in order to establish (1) whether the entity or gifts of entity interests are excluded from the donor's estate, and (2) whether gifts of those interests qualify as completed gifts for tax purposes under IRC Section 2503(b). For there to be a bona fide sale, there must be a legitimate **nontax reason** behind the creation of the entity, which occurs as an arms-length transaction between a willing buyer and a willing seller. The nontax reason cannot be just a theoretical justification but an actual motivation.

In determining whether the nontax reason exists, the following factors may be considered:

1. The taxpayer's **legal and financial condition** on both sides of the transaction;
2. The taxpayer's **financial dependence** on distributions from the partnership;
3. The taxpayer's **commingling** of partnership funds with the taxpayer's own;
4. The taxpayer's actual **failure to transfer** the property to the partnership;
5. Discounting the **value** of the partnership interest relative to the value of the property contributed; and
6. The taxpayer's **advanced age or poor health** when the partnership was formed.

An **arm's-length transaction** occurs when mutual legitimate and significant nontax reasons exist for the transaction and the transaction is carried out in a way in which **unrelated parties to a business transaction** would deal with each other.

In the case of gifted interests, in determining whether the gifts were present interests, the court will review whether the donees obtained **use, possession, or enjoyment** from the FLP interest or income from those interests within the meaning of IRC Section 2503(b), which is required to establish an annual exclusion gift.

CHAPTER FIVE – ESTATE AND FIDUCIARY TAXES

Q & A

Question 1: What is the **basic exclusion amount** for the calendar year 2016?
Answer: The basic exclusion amount for 2016 is $5,450,000 for determining the amount of the unified credit against estate tax under IRC § 2010.

Question 2: What is the **lifetime gift tax exclusion** amount for the calendar year 2016?
Answer: The lifetime gift tax exclusion amount is $5,450,000 for the credit against gift tax under IRC § 2505.

Question 3: What is the **fiduciary income tax rate** for calendar year 2016?
Answer: Fiduciary income taxes for 2016 are 39.6% on all undistributed income over $12,400 as reported on Form 1041. In certain circumstances, the 3.8% Medicare tax could also apply to trusts with passive income.

Question 4: How did the **American Taxpayer Relief Act** of 2012 affect the current law?
Answer: The 2012 Estate and Gift Tax Law extended most of the prior provisions of the estate and gift tax law. The top estate and gift tax rate, however, increased to 40%.

2016 FEDERAL TAX RATES

Federal Capital Gains

Short-term (one year or less)*	Ordinary rate
Long-term (longer than one year)*	15-20%

*Capital gain rates may be subject to an additional 3.8% Medicare tax.

Federal Trust and Estate Income Tax

Taxable income	Tax
More than	+ % on excess
$0	15%
$2,550	25%
$5,950	28%
$9,050	33%
$12,400	39.6%

Estate, Gift, and Generation-Skipping Transfer Tax

Gift Tax Annual Exclusion

In 2016, each individual may transfer up to **$14,000 per person per year** to any number of beneficiaries (family or nonfamily) without paying gift tax or "using up" any available applicable exclusion amount.

Applicable Exclusion

$5,450,000 in 2016

The applicable exclusion protects lifetime taxable gifts and transfers upon death from gift and estate tax, respectively.

Under "portability" rules, a surviving spouse's applicable exclusion may be increased by the unused exclusion of a prior spouse who died on or after January 1, 2011. The "portability election" is made on a Form 706 estate tax return for the deceased spouse, which is due nine months after the decedent's death. Portability is discussed in further detail below.

All decedents whose estate exceeds the applicable exclusion amount must file a 706 estate tax return. This return must show all values includible in the decedent's gross estate on the date of death, including any methods for computing valuation discounts. The return is due nine months after the decedent's date of death. For taxable estates, **date-of-death basis information** must also be provided to beneficiaries by the executor or trustee in order for the IRS and beneficiaries to monitor the step-up in basis upon the decedent's death pursuant to the basis consistency rules by the use of Form 8971. Form 8971 is to be filed with the IRS and provided to each beneficiary no later than the earlier of (1) 30 days after the date upon which the 706 is required to be filed, or (2) 30 days after the 706 is filed with the IRS.

Generation-Skipping Transfer (GST) Tax Exemption

$5,450,000 in 2016

Estate, Gift, and GST Tax Rate

40% for any amount exceeding the applicable exclusion/ GST exemption.

FACTORING IN THE 3.8% MEDICARE TAX ON INVESTMENT INCOME FOR INDIVIDUALS AND TRUSTS

Q & A

Question 1: **Who** does the Medicare tax apply to?
Answer: The Medicare tax applies to individuals, estates, and trusts with investment income.

Question 2: **How much** is the Medicare tax?
Answer: The Medicare tax is 3.8%, which is in addition to regular income tax and alternative minimum taxes.

Question 3: **What** is the Medicare tax based on?
Answer: The Medicare tax is based on a calculation of net investment income applied to various pecuniary thresholds and is applicable to trusts after considering both fiduciary accounting income and distributable net income.

Question 4: What is the **threshold for trust income** in 2016?
Answer: Any trust that has in excess of $12,400 for the taxable year of 2016 may be subject to the Medicare tax.

Overview

The Health Care and Education Reconciliation Act of 2010 included an additional 3.8% tax on "net investment income" (NII) that went into effect January 1, 2013.

The tax applies to individuals, estates, and trusts, and is in addition to regular income tax and the AMT (alternative minimum tax).

The term "net investment income" consists of **three categories** of investment income: gross income from interest, dividends, annuities, royalties, and rents; gross income from a passive activity or a trade or business of trading in financial instruments or commodities; and net gain "to the extent taken into account in computing taxable income" from the disposition of certain property. There are special rules regarding the disposition of S corporation stock or partnership interests.

The following are adjustments to NII: (1) the "flow through" treatment of S corporations and partnerships and (2) the exception for business gain. This is intended to be a pro-taxpayer provision, shielding from the 3.8% surtax net gain attributable to an active trade or business in which the taxpayer is a material participant.

Retirement plan distributions, compensation income/salary, income on the exercise of compensatory options, and vesting of restricted stock are excluded from the calculation of net investment income.

For an individual, the 3.8% tax is imposed on the **lesser of** (i) NII, or (ii) the excess of MAGI (Modified Adjusted Gross Income) over a certain threshold amount. For trusts and estates, the 3.8% tax is imposed on the lesser of (i) undistributed NII, or (ii) the excess of adjusted gross income over the dollar amount at which the highest tax bracket is reached for estates and trusts. That amount is $12,400 for 2016.

We have always had rules to figure out what income has been retained or distributed. Those are the **Distributable Net Income (DNI) rules**.

Distributable Net Income (DNI) is the measure that limits the amount of the distributions from estates and trusts that the beneficiaries thereof will have to include in income. Also, DNI limits the amount that estates and trusts can claim as a deduction for such distributions. I.R.C. §643(a).

A determination of both **fiduciary accounting income (FAI)** and DNI is necessary to compute the distribution deduction pursuant to §651 or §661 and the resulting gross income to the beneficiaries under §652 or §662. FAI is a determination made based on the Uniform Principal and Income Act or other applicable state law, the governing instrument, and any other relevant matters as to the amount of income the trust or estate has earned in a particular year. These issues are most relevant for determining the rights of a beneficiary with respect to trust income. They are also relevant in determining the distribution deduction and the beneficiary's gross income from distributions.

DNI and FAI most often are not the same in a given year because their functions are different. FAI is concerned with equitable concepts of determining the amount of income and principal between income beneficiaries and remaindermen. DNI is concerned with determining the appropriate amount of tax to be borne by the trust or estate and its beneficiaries. Thus, an item that may be subject to federal income tax will not necessarily be "income" for state law purposes (e.g., capital gains). Similarly, an expense that may be deductible for income tax purposes may not be charged in full against "income" for state law purposes (e.g., all of the fiduciary fees).

The question is how a trust determines how much of its NII has been distributed and how much is undistributed. IRS regulations provide answers and examples to assist with analyzing and answering this question.

PORTABILITY

Q & A

Question 1: What is **portability**?
Answer: Portability is the ability under the federal tax code to take the unused exclusion amount of a deceased spouse and transfer it to the surviving spouse for federal estate and gift tax purposes.

Question 2: How is portability of the unused exclusion amount used or **applied** to the surviving spouse's estate?
Answer: In order to transfer the deceased spouse's unused exclusion amount **(DSUEA)**, the decedent's personal representative must file a 706 estate tax return and allocate it to the surviving spouse.

Question 3: **Who** may take advantage of the portability rules?
Answer: A surviving spouse.

Question 4: What is the **limit** of the DSUEA?
Answer: In 2016, the maximum amount that could potentially be ported to the surviving spouse is $5,450,000.

"Portability" refers to the federal estate tax concept of being able to transfer (or "port") a deceased spouse's unused exclusion ("DSUE") amount over to the surviving spouse (one should note, however, that there is no portability of the GST exemption). To take advantage of portability, the executor must make the portability election on a "complete and properly-prepared" estate tax return which is timely-filed.

With the advent of portability, **new terms** have been created:

- **Basic Exclusion Amount ("BEA")**. The amount an individual can pass free of federal estate tax ($5,450,000 in 2016).
- **Deceased Spouse Unused Exclusion ("DSUE") Amount**. The deceased spouse's unused applicable exclusion amount at the time of the decedent's death that can be ported over to the surviving spouse.
- **Applicable Exclusion Amount**. The BEA plus the ported DSUE amount.

There were many changes made by the regulations, some of which are addressed below.

In order to make the election, the executor must file a **"timely-filed" Form 706** federal estate tax return, without regard to size of gross estate and taxable gifts. Generally, a timely-filed return is due nine months after death, with an available six-month extension. Once the election is made and the time for filing has expired, then portability is "irrevocable." However, it is possible to revoke the election up to the nine-month (or, if extended, fifteen-month) period. No portability election is available for Non-Resident Non-Citizens.

The Form 706 being filed for portability purposes must be a **"complete and properly-prepared" return**.

However, there are special rules if estate is a "smaller estate," meaning that no Form 706 is required and the return is only be filed for the purpose of electing portability. For these returns, there are simplified filing requirements available which allow for rounding values to the nearest $250,000 (although this approach may not be recommended). In addition, the return must also contain a computation of the DSUE amount.

The **computation** of the DSUE amount can be complicated. The executor adds the DSUE amount of prior deceased spouses if the decedent used such prior spouses' DSUE amounts for lifetime gifts. The regulations provide that the DSUE amount is the DSUE amount from "Last Deceased Spouse," plus the DSUE amount from prior deceased spouses if that amount was applied against prior taxable gifts made by the decedent.

The **Last Deceased Spouse** – who is the last deceased spouse? The regulations clarified that it is the last person that the decedent was married to who had passed away prior to the time of the decedent's death. The regulations also clarified that if the decedent married and divorced a person, the divorce would have no effect on the last deceased spouse. For example, assume that H1 was married to W. H1 dies. W marries and subsequently divorces H2. H2 dies (after the divorce). H1 is W's last deceased spouse.

A **Prior Deceased Spouse** is a predeceased spouse who is not the decedent's Last Deceased Spouse. This would occur in a multiple marriage situation, and is primarly relevant only if the decedent used any of such prior deceased spouse's DSUE amount during life for gifting purposes.

The regulations also set forth the **ordering rule** of how to apply the various amounts for the purpose of gift and estate tax. It is now clear that you use the ported DSUE amount first, and then apply the surviving spouse's BEA. The benefits of electing portability prompt the inquiry as to why an executor would **choose NOT to make the election**. The answer comes down to a cost/benefit analysis of the matter. With the required filing of the 706, there is an expense for the preparation of the same, both in the time and effort required to obtain the necessary information for the return and in the actual legal and accounting time to prepare the return. If the surviving spouse is likely to never need the DSUE amount due to the value of the surviving spouse's estate being substantially less than the BEA, then the executor may view these expenses as outweighing the benefit of porting the DSUE amount.

Portability, however, is **not always the answer** when it comes to estate planning, and using **a traditional by-pass trust still has great benefit**. A traditional by-pass trust allows for the following benefits:

- Coordinates asset management for the surviving spouse;
- Provides asset protection for the surviving spouse via spendthrift trust protection;
- Allows for disposition control by the deceased spouse (i.e., preventing the surviving spouse from diverting the assets);
- Allows for use of the deceased spouse's GST exemption (since the GST exemption is not portable);

- Protects accretions in value from estate tax upon the surviving spouse's death since it is not includible in the surviving spouse's estate;
- Provides for more control by the deceased spouse in second marriages and blended families;
- Limits disclosure of the deceased spouse's estate tax return to the surviving spouse (i.e., a desire for privacy); and
- Provides protection in using the BEA of the deceased spouse rather than porting it to the surviving spouse, who could lose the DSUE amount by remarriage and the death of a subsequent spouse.

When drafting **marital agreements**, the drafter should consider the following: who pays for the 706 return preparation to make the election; how to enforce filing of election; and, if a client has a DSUE amount from a deceased spouse, how to protect against the last deceased spouse rule.

The drafter should consider drafting provisions in the Prenuptial Agreement, Last Will and Testament, and Revocable Trust to address these issues.

ESTATE PLANNING FOR SAME-SEX MARRIAGES

Q & A

Question 1: Are spouses of a same-sex marriage deemed to **hold property** as husband and wife?

Answer: Yes. Pursuant to the *Windsor* case (133 S.Ct. 2884 [2013]) and IRS Rev. Rul. 2013-17, the term "husband and wife" should be interpreted to include same-sex spouses for federal law purposes when certain requirements are met. *Obergefell v. Hodges* (135 S.Ct. 2584 [2015]) legalized same-sex marriage throughout the United States.

Question 2: How do same-sex partners **qualify** for treatment as husband and wife?

Answer: The terms "husband and wife," "husband," and "wife" include an individual married to a person of the same sex if they were lawfully married in a state whose laws authorize the marriage of two individuals of the same sex.

Question 3: Do the provisions of the **Internal Revenue Code** that apply to opposite sex spouses also apply to same-sex marriage?

Answer: Yes. Pursuant to *Windsor* and IRS Rev. Rul. 2013-17, the terms "spouse" and "husband and wife" include an individual married to a person of the same sex if the individuals were lawfully married under state law.

Question 4: When did the same-sex marriage rulings become **applicable**?

Answer: The *Windsor* ruling was applied prospectively as of September 16, 2013, and *Obergefell* as of June 26, 2015.

Question 5: Does the *Windsor* ruling apply to **employee benefits** under ERISA?

Answer: Yes. The U.S. Labor Department and the IRS have stated that the ruling is applicable to the employee benefit plans of same-sex couples.

IRS Revenue Ruling 2013-17

Many provisions of the Code make reference to the marital status of taxpayers. Until the decision of the United States Supreme Court in *United States v. Windsor* (2013), the Service interpreted section 3 of the Defense of Marriage Act (DOMA) as prohibiting it from recognizing same-sex marriages. In *Windsor*, the Supreme Court held that **section 3 of DOMA is unconstitutional** because it violates the principles of equal protection.

Consistent with the statutory context, the Supreme Court's decision in *Windsor*, Revenue Ruling 58-66, and effective tax administration generally, the Service concluded that, for federal tax purposes, the terms "husband and wife," "husband," and "wife" include an individual married to a person of the same sex if they were lawfully married in a state whose laws authorize the marriage of two individuals of the same sex, and the term "marriage" includes such marriages of individuals of the same sex. Under this rule, individuals of the same sex will be considered to be **lawfully married** under the Code as long as they were married in a state whose laws authorize the marriage of two individuals of the same sex, even if they are domiciled in a state that does not recognize the validity of same-sex marriages.

For federal tax purposes, the terms "spouse," "husband and wife," "husband," and "wife" **do not include** individuals (whether of the opposite sex or the same sex) who have entered into a registered domestic partnership, civil union, or other similar formal relationship recognized under state law that is not denominated as a marriage under the laws of that state, and the term "marriage" does not include such formal relationships.

The *Obergefell* decision legalized same-sex marriage throughout the United States. All states are required to issue marriage licenses to same-sex couples and recognize same-sex marriages from other jurisdictions.

FIDUCIARY ACCESS TO DIGITAL ASSETS

Missouri is formulating rules for the access to digital assets by means of a specific statutory act. The purpose of this act is to **vest fiduciaries with the authority to access**, control, or copy digital assets and accounts. The goal of the act is to remove barriers to a fiduciary's access to electronic records and to establish substantive rules for fiduciaries, probate courts, trust companies, banks, and agencies with regard to their access and transfer such assets.

The act proposes to address different types of fiduciaries: **personal representatives** of decedents' estates, **conservators** for protected persons, **agents** acting pursuant to a power of attorney, and **trustees**. The act applies only to fiduciaries that act in compliance with their fiduciary powers. It distinguishes the authority of fiduciaries, which exercise authority subject to this statute only on behalf of the account holder, from any other efforts to access the digital assets. Family members or friends may seek such access, but, unless they are fiduciaries, their efforts are subject to other state laws and are not covered by this act.

POWERS OF APPOINTMENT

Q & A

Question 1: What is a power of appointment?

Answer: A power of appointment is **a power exercisable in favor of any one or more of the permissible appointees**, designated under the governing instrument, establishing the power and limits of the power. A power of appointment establishes a power that enables a **powerholder, acting in a nonfiduciary capacity, to designate a recipient** of an ownership interest over the appointive property. The term does not include a power of attorney.

Question 2: What is a **general power** of appointment?

Answer: A general power of appointment is a power of appointment exercisable in favor of the powerholder, the powerholder's estate, a creditor of the powerholder, or a creditor of the powerholder's estate.

Question 3: Who is a **donor**?

Answer: A donor is a person who **creates** the power of appointment.

Question 4: What is a non-general or **limited power** of appointment?

Answer: A non-general or limited power of appointment is a power of appointment that is not a general power of appointment.

Question 5: What is a **presently exercisable** power of appointment?

Answer: A "presently exercisable power of appointment" is a power of appointment exercisable by the powerholder at the **relevant time**. The term includes a power of appointment not exercisable (1) until the occurrence of a specified event, (2) the satisfaction of an ascertainable standard, (3) the passage of a specified time only after the occurrence of the specified event, (4) the satisfaction of the ascertainable standard, or (5) the passage of the specified time, and does not include a power exercisable only at the powerholder's death.

Question 6: What is a **taker in default of appointment**?

Answer: A taker in default of appointment is a person who takes all or part of the appointive property to the extent the powerholder does **not effectively exercise the power** of appointment.

A power of appointment may be granted under a **trust, will, or other instrument** enabling a powerholder to exercise and designate **who may receive the benefits** of specific property rights or assets which are held and controlled under the terms and conditions of the governing instrument.

The power of appointment may be general in nature or limited, depending on the terms contained in the **governing instrument**.

Powers of appointment may be drafted to be **flexible or very limited**, depending on the donor's desires. In the event a power of appointment is not exercised by a powerholder, a well-drafted instrument should designate how the property is to be distributed in default of the exercise. Accordingly, the governing instrument will **direct who will take the**

property interest in default of the exercise of the power of appointment.

The granting of a power of appointment and the exercise of a power of appointment must be analyzed, not only from a **transfer of property** point of view, but also a **tax** point of view. A general power of appointment typically results in a **taxable inclusion** of the property to the powerholder's estate, while a non-general power of appointment may circumvent such a taxable inclusion.

Powers of appointment are typically used to allow a powerholder to **pick and choose** from a pool of permissible appointees who should receive the benefit of certain property interests. This decision may be based on **unforeseen circumstances** that the donor was unaware of when he or she created the power. For example, a spouse or child may be given the ability to appoint property to certain children or descendants whose specific need was not previously ascertained.

A financial power of attorney should be drafted to allow an attorney in fact to exercise powers of appointment on behalf of the power holder.

The Missouri Bar is proposing a new statute that will address all of the issues surrounding the use of a power of appointment that should become effective on August 28, 2016, under R.S.Mo. Section 456.970.

CHAPTER SEVEN – TRUST ADMINISTRATION

Question 1: What is the difference between **a probate administration and a trust** administration?
Answer: A probate administration requires the probate **court to oversee** the management and distribution of a person's estate. The court must oversee and order the transfer of a person's assets passing through a will or to the person's heirs if no will was made. A trust is generally administered without court involvement and allows the trustee to transfer the trust assets under the terms and conditions of the trust agreement.

Question 2: How does a **successor trustee** take over a trust and the trust assets?
Answer: A successor trustee named in a trust must adhere to the terms of the agreement in order to take control of the trust estate; this includes formally accepting the trusteeship, typically by a **written acceptance**, and coordinating the control and transfer of the trust assets with the financial institutions where the trust assets are held.

Question 3: What assets are **managed** by a trustee?
Answer: All of the assets **titled in the name** of a trust or **transferred** into the trust by deed, beneficiary designation, or assignment.

Question 4: How long does a trust administration last?
Answer: The trustee must take charge of all of the trust assets, file notice of the trust administration to establish a six-month creditor claim period, inventory the estate, pay any taxes or expenses, liquidate or consolidate assets,

coordinate with a probate estate, prepare a settlement of all accounts, make distributions, and get receipts from the beneficiaries. This process could take one year or more **depending on the complexity** of the estate. If sub-trusts are created, a sub-trust may continue for many years.

Question 5: How is the trustee **paid**?
Answer: The trustee will receive a fee as indicated in the trust agreement. A **reasonable** fee would be based on a percentage of the total asset value, for example, 1%.

TRUST ADMINISTRATION

A named successor trustee has numerous responsibilities in the administration of a decedent's trust upon the settlor's death.

The successor trustee must first **accept the position** as trustee. Afterward, the administration begins with informing the family or beneficiaries of their position and assisting them as needed. This could include helping with making **funeral** arrangements, obtaining a cemetery marker, ordering an announcement in the paper, arranging for a memorial service, and notifying friends and relatives.

The trustee must review all **debts and claims** and communicate with the claimants in order to ascertain the validity of the claims. It is recommended that the trustee publish **notice in a newspaper** in order to establish a bar to and an expiration of the claims period (six months after first publication), which is specifically authorized by statute.

The trustee should ascertain the names, addresses, ages, dates of birth, and Social Security Numbers for all permissible **distributees** and qualified **beneficiaries**. Additionally, the trustee should ascertain the name and address of the guardians of any minors and assist with the establishment of guardianship proceedings if necessary.

The Missouri statutes require that the trustee send **notices to the trust beneficiaries** within 120 days of the settlor's death. This provides the beneficiaries with the necessary information to enforce the beneficiary's rights regarding the trust and is part of the checks-and-balances system on the trustee. The trustee must give a copy of the trust document to each beneficiary requesting a copy. If any of the beneficiaries are under 21, another copy of the notice will need to be sent to the beneficiary when the beneficiary attains the age of 21.

The trustee should make sure to keep all back-up trustees fully informed throughout the process and order at least 12 certified **death certificates** from the funeral home.

The trustee should notify various persons and institutions after the settlor's death, including:

1. The **attorney** who prepared the trust document. He/she should be aware of the death in case the trustee, beneficiaries or family members need to call with questions.

2. If the decedent was a party to a **lawsuit** at death, the attorney handling such lawsuit.

3. The **bank** so the trustee can start writing checks. The bank will probably want to see a certified

death certificate, a copy of the trust document, and the trustee's personal identification. If applicable, the decedent's joint bank account should remain open for approximately one year.

4. **Social Security.**

5. Life **insurance companies**, **retirement plans**, pension plans, associations, and any others that will provide a death benefit.

With regard to **retirement accounts**, the trustee should review retirement accounts and their beneficiary designations. If any of the beneficiaries on retirement accounts are charities, they need to be cashed out prior to September 30 the year after the date of death to assure that a designated beneficiary status has been established under the Internal Revenue Code regulations. The trustee must also ascertain if the decedent took the Required Minimum Distribution for the year of his or her death.

The trustee should submit an application to the Missouri Department of Insurance Life Policy Locator Service in order to ascertain whether the decedent had any life insurance policies.

The trustee should notify the **credit reporting agencies**, Equifax, Experian, and TransUnion of the death of decedent to prevent theft of the decedent's identity.

The trustee should notify the **Secretary of State** if the decedent was the Managing Member of a Family Limited Partnership (required within thirty days of date of death to avoid penalty) and amend the partnership Articles.

If the decedent had any rights in **other trusts** (e.g., if the decedent was a current income beneficiary, a trustee, or had a power of appointment), the taxable includibility and control of the disposition of those trusts must be reviewed.

The trustee should secure and **inventory** all of the trust property, especially real estate, and ascertain date of death **values** for all assets and obtain appraisals, if necessary or appropriate. The trustee must make sure he/she has keys to all homes and vehicles, make arrangements to keep the utilities on (or turn them off), and make sure that the insurance is in force and the mortgage is paid. The trustee must start a list of all assets. In order to ensure a complete inventory of estate assets, the trustee should run a search on the Missouri Unclaimed Property website, http://www.treasurer.mo.gov/mainUCP.asp, as well as in the Unclaimed Property division of any other state in which the decedent resided during life, to see if the decedent has any unclaimed property.

The trustee must collect any **bills** and start a **detailed ledger** of accounts payable and income received. This is a necessary part of the trustee's duties in being able to properly account to the beneficiaries for all trust transactions.

During the decedent's life, the decedent's Social Security Number was used for the trust. However, after the trust becomes irrevocable, a **new federal tax identification number** must be obtained for the trust. Once received from the IRS, the trust assets must be adjusted to reflect the new tax identification number so that information is properly reported for tax purposes.

The trustee must also contact an accountant, as there are several issues to review. The decedent will owe a **final 1040 income tax return**, which will be due on April 15 in the year following the decedent's death, for the income made prior to death. The trust will owe a **1041 income tax return**, which will also be due on April 15 in the year following the decedent's death. The 1041 is filed under the new federal tax identification number and will reflect the post-death trust income. In looking at the post-death income tax issues, the potential for making a Section 645 election should be reviewed with the CPA in order to achieve the best tax results for the estate as a whole.

If a **Form 706 estate tax return** is due for a taxable estate (meaning an estate with a gross value of $5,450,000.00 or more), or if a **portability election** is being made by the surviving spouse in a non-taxable estate, the 706 (or the request for an automatic six-month extension) must be filed nine months after the decedent's date of death. The failure to file in a taxable estate will result in an automatic 25% penalty, plus interest, on the amount due. In a non-taxable estate, the failure to timely make the portability election will result in the loss of the option to the surviving spouse and in the inability to port over the deceased spouse's unused exemption amount.

The trustee should obtain signed **waivers**, if necessary, and review **disclaimers** if made by beneficiaries within nine months of the date of death. The trustee should review and consider any **post-mortem planning**, such as alternative asset valuation options, funding of trusts as provided for in the estate plan, and establish timelines for the distribution of assets.

With regard to probate, the trustee should have the attorney **admit the decedent's Last Will and Testament with the Probate Court** in the county where the decedent was domiciled at the time of death. In Missouri, the Will must be admitted to the Probate Court (not just filed) within one year of death in order to be valid. There is a court filing fee for the admission, which varies by county. If assets are located that require probate, there are different options on how to proceed with the court process depending upon the value of the assets requiring probate.

The trustee also has the **option to file the trust agreement with the Probate Court** in order to shorten the period in which the trust could be contested from two years to six months. However, filing the trust for this purpose will require the opening of a full probate estate, and it will also make the trust public record.

The trustee should make a **final accounting and trust settlement** of all assets inventoried, income earned, and bills paid. The trustee should give a copy of the settlement to all beneficiaries before the property is distributed (and if there are sub-trusts, the final distributions will not occur until the sub-trusts are terminated). Upon the **consent** and approval of all beneficiaries, the trustee may distribute the property, making sure to get **a receipt** signed by each beneficiary (or the trustee of a sub-trust, if applicable) stating that he/she has received the property and that the trustee is released from any further liability regarding the distribution.

Estate Planning: The Fundamental Concepts Under Missouri Law

SUPPLEMENTAL MATERIAL 2018 UPDATE

1. What changes occurred in the federal estate, gift and generation skipping transfer tax laws under the 2017 Tax Cut and Jobs Act?
2. How long does the new tax law apply to a person's estate?
3. What will happen if Congress does not renew the tax law after 2025?
4. Can a marital QTIP trust still be used to defer estate taxes until the death of the surviving spouse?
5. Do a decedent's assets which are includible in his or her taxable estate still receive a step-up in basis at the decedent's death regarding capital gains?
6. Is the income generated in a trust affected by the new income tax rates?
7. How does the new tax law affect charitable planning for estates?
8. How does the new law tax affect transfers to children?

9. How does the new tax law affect retirement planning and the transfer of retirement plans within a person's estate plan?
10. How does the new tax law affect the transfer of business interests within a person's estate plan?
11. How does the new tax law affect the use of insurance in an estate plan?
12. May a conservation easement still be used for estate planning purposes?
13. May an irrevocable trust still be decanted?
14. May powers of appointment still be used for estate planning?
15. What changes have occurred in the Missouri trust or probate laws?
16. What estate planning techniques are recommended as a result of the new tax law and Missouri trust law changes?

1. What changes occurred in the federal estate, gift and generation skipping transfer tax laws under the 2017 Tax Cut and Jobs Act?

Under the 2017 Tax Cut and Jobs Act ("Act"), the current law has been doubled in consideration of the CPI (consumer price index) resulting in the current **estate, gift, and generation skipping transfer tax** exclusions each being approximately $11,200,000 in 2018. Prior to the new tax act, the exclusion allowed a U.S. citizen to transfer $5,600,000 as of January 1, 2018. Accordingly, each married couple may transfer approximately $22,400,000 at their death or during their life. These transfers may be to their descendants or other "skip" persons for generation-skipping purposes.

Therefore, any lifetime or death transfers that do not exceed these amounts will not incur federal transfer taxes. By way of example, if a person transferred $11,000,000 through their estate during the effective dates of the Act, the estate tax basic exclusion, i.e. "credit," and generation skipping transfer tax exclusion would offset any estate tax obligation. It should be noted that the basic exclusion amount for non-resident aliens remains at $60,000 thereby granting a $13,000 lifetime credit.

Additionally, the Act maintained the requirement that the executor/trustee of an estate that is taxable and required to file a 706 estate tax return must **report the basis** of all assets transferred to the beneficiaries. This requirement is satisfied by the executor filing Form 8971 so that the IRS may track the capital gains step up or carry over attributable to the beneficiaries on the assets received at the decedent's death.

In addition, the **annual gift tax exclusion** has increased to $15,000 per individual recipient (subject to CPI increases in the future). Therefore, any combination of gifts under this amount, per year per individual, does not need to be reported. If an individual is gifted more than the annual exclusion amount, the donor is still required to report the gift on a 709 gift tax return for the taxable year in which the gift was made. This reporting enables the IRS to keep track of all taxable gifts which will need to be incorporated into an individual's taxable estate at their death. By way of example, if a person made a gift in 2018 of $115,000 to an individual, a 709 gift tax return should be filed for the 2018 taxable year showing a $100,000 gift in excess of the annual gift tax exclusion of $15,000.

2. How long does the new tax law apply to a person's estate?

The terms of the Tax Cut and Jobs Act will continue through **December 31, 2025**, after which it is scheduled to sunset.

3. What will happen if Congress does not renew the tax law after 2025?

In the event Congress does not renew the Act the estate, gift, and generation skipping tax will automatically revert to the amount it would have been (as adjusted for inflation) under the old law. By way of example, if on January 1, 2026 the Act is not renewed, the exclusion amount will be $5,000,000 adjusted for inflation for each U.S. citizen. In theory, the IRS could argue that any transfers that were previously made under the Act could be "**clawed back**" into an individual's estate. This argument, however, may be unconstitutional since the taxpayer would have relied upon the then current law at the time the transfer was made. Therefore, the taxpayer should be able to rely on the terms of the Tax Cut and Jobs Act until December 31, 2025; the current consensus is that Congress did not intend for a claw back to occur.

4. Can a marital QTIP trust still be used to defer estate taxes until the death of the surviving spouse?

Under the terms of the Act, most of the estate tax law provisions have remained the same, including the **unlimited marital deduction** pursuant to Internal Revenue Code ("I.R.C.") Section 2056. Under this provision a spouse may transfer an unlimited amount to a spouse during their life or at their death. This transfer may be outright, in trust, or a combination of both. In most cases, a transfer in trust will be preferred because of the benefits which a trust may offer. For example, a marital trust can allow the spouse to be the trustee and permits the spouse to receive all the income, with the discretion to encroach upon principal for the spouse's health, education, maintenance, support and comfort. Additionally, when the discretion to make transfers of principal is combined with a spendthrift clause, this will grant protection of the trust assets from the reach of the spouse's creditors. A marital trust may be established to provide for the direct distribution of the remaining trust after the spouse's death or grant the spouse the ability to appoint where the distribution will go after their death (e.g., to the spouse's descendants) in the proportions deemed best by the spouse.

A qualified terminal interest trust ("**QTIP trust**") is a specific type of marital trust authorized under the I.R.C. Section 2056(b)(7). A QTIP trust mandates the distribution of all income to the spouse but allows for variation of the terms regarding the principal distribution. This type of trust will qualify for the unlimited marital deduction, and the trust assets will be automatically included in the taxable estate of the surviving spouse. If a QTIP Trust is desired it should be noted that a surviving spouse must make an election on the deceased spouse's 706 estate tax return in order to make use of the provision. A partial QTIP election may still be made if it would be beneficial.

In the event an individual desires to transfer an IRA to a spouse but does not wish for the surviving spouse to be given the power to withdraw the entire balance, a transfer of the IRA through a QTIP trust is still a possible solution. Under this strategy, the trust must provide the surviving spouse with the right to be paid the greater of the trust income or the required minimum distributions (RMDs) based upon the spouse's life expectancy. It should be noted that if the spouse lives long enough most of the IRA assets will likely have been distributed to the surviving spouse.

The Act did not change a surviving spouse's ability to use his or her **deceased spousal unused exemption amount** (DESUA), which is commonly referred to as a portability election. This strategy allows a surviving spouse to carry over, or "port," the unused basic exclusion amount that the deceased spouse did not use. In this way the surviving spouse may use both his or her and the deceased spouse's unused estate tax credit at the time of the surviving spouse's death. A **portability election** must be made on the deceased spouse's 706 estate tax return. If both spouses died in 2018, this strategy will ensure that a married couple may use both basic exclusion amounts and be able to pass $22,400,000 at the surviving spouse's death. It should be noted that the portability election does not apply to the generation skipping transfer tax exemption; accordingly, specific planning for the transfer of assets to skip persons (e.g., grandchildren) must be reviewed and analyzed.

5. Do a decedent's assets which are includible in his or her taxable estate still receive a step-up in basis at the decedent's death regarding capital gains?

In addition to the estate tax provisions maintained under the new Act, Congress has retained the **step up in cost basis at death** pursuant to I.R.C. section 1014. Generally, any assets, other than retirement assets, qualified plan assets and annuities, will have their basis increased to the value on the date of the decedent's death. Accordingly, an individual U.S. citizen may now transfer $11,200,000 of assets at their death, and if they are non-qualified assets, the decedent's estate will receive a full step up in basis, to the date of death value.

As a result of the new estate tax provisions, some people may wish to transfer all or a majority of their assets to a spouse through the use of an outright bequest, a marital QTIP trust, or by granting a general power of appointment, thereby allowing the spouse the use of the assets during the spouse's life but also gaining a step up in basis for capital gains purposes at the surviving spouse's death. As a result, in the event the surviving spouse's gross estate **was valued at less than $11,200,000;** after receiving their spouse's marital transfer, the couple's entire estate could be transferred both estate and capital gains free at the second death.

In the event the surviving spouse does not want all of the deceased spouse's assets in their taxable estate and desired to shelter all or part of the estate from estate tax inclusion, a marital trust could provide the surviving spouse with the **power to disclaim** all or part of the marital trust. The disclaimer could allow for an outright distribution or a distribution to a standard residuary trust (credit shelter). In order for this strategy to work, the surviving spouse must legally and timely elect to disclaim a certain amount from the marital trust and allow the assets disclaimed to be distributed under the terms of the trust instrument without the surviving spouse's direction.

For example, a spouse could disclaim all or part of the marital trust, allowing such disclaimed amount to automatically be transferred to a residuary trust for the benefit of the surviving spouse and then to the descendants of the deceased spouse. This strategy would allow the surviving spouse to dictate how much of the deceased spouse's tax credit should be used and allocate the portion of the estate assets which would receive a step up in basis. A qualified disclaimer must be made by the beneficiary no later than nine (9) months after the decedent's death (or after a trust becomes irrevocable) in order to avoid any tax consequences to the beneficiary.

6. Is the income generated in a trust affected by the new income tax rates?

Under the Act, Congress lowered the **marginal income tax rates** for most taxpayers, thereby reducing the top marginal rate to 37%. The new rates are applicable to the taxation of irrevocable trusts, such as marital and residuary trusts. If a trust accumulates income and does not distribute it to the beneficiaries in any taxable year, the trust must file a **1041 fiduciary tax return** and report the income which the trust generated. In this event, the trust must pay income taxes at the top marginal rate of 37% on all income over $13,200.

Based upon the punitive income tax rates applicable to trusts that accumulate income, in most circumstances the best strategy generally is for a trustee to distribute the net income directly to the beneficiaries. This distribution would allow the beneficiaries to report the trust income (based on an informational K-1 given by the trustee to the beneficiary) on the beneficiary's personal 1040 income tax return and thereby pay the income tax at the beneficiary's "lower" marginal rate.

The Act did change some of the **miscellaneous administrative deductions** which a trustee may take on either a 706 estate tax return or a 1041 income tax return for administrative purposes (e.g., fees and administrative losses), which would have little effect upon an individual's estate planning process. Many deductions within a trust administration, such as the deduction for IRD (income in respect of a decedent), were maintained under the Act. It should be noted that excess deductions within a trust may not be passed out to beneficiaries except in the year of the trust's termination. All of these deductions should be reviewed with the CPA assisting in a trust's 1041 fiduciary income tax return.

7. How does the new tax law affect charitable planning for estates?

For **charitable planning**, the Act allows an individual who is over the age of 70 ½ to make a direct transfer and distribution from their IRA to a qualified charity thereby fulfilling their RMD (required minimum distribution). This strategy will qualify the charitable distribution as a charitable deduction; as a result, the distribution will not need to be reported as taxable income to the donor for the year of the transfer. This strategy may also be used with an inherited IRA. Before taking advantage of this charitable strategy, an individual should consult with their CPA to calculate the benefit (based upon their use of the standard deduction verses the use of an itemized deduction on their 1040 tax return).

Finally, the Act increased the limit of personal charitable deductions to 60% of AGI (adjustable gross income) for any taxable year. The Act continues the five (5) year carry forward of unused charitable deductions. Accordingly, if an individual desired to make a charitable contribution, they may wish to bunch the donation up in one taxable year in order to take advantage of itemizing the donation(s) on their 1040 tax return. Such a distribution could be made to a Donor Advised Fund (DAF) which would allow the donor to direct charitable distributions over a series of years. The Act did change some of the miscellaneous deductions for income tax purposes, and these should be reviewed with a CPA in order to determine the applicability to an individual's taxation situation.

8. How does the new law tax affect transfers to children?

The "Kiddie Tax" rules, pertaining to the income tax attributable to **minor's accounts**, were modified under the Act, changing the ages and rates of taxation. The new rules apply to children's accounts until the age of 19 or the age of 24 if the child is a student. The tax rate was changed to mirror the tax rates attributable to trusts. An individual who has established minor's accounts should review the new rules with their CPA.

9. How does the new tax law affect retirement planning and the transfer of retirement plans within a person's estate plan?

The Act did not change an individual's ability to convert and rollover an employer sponsored plan (e.g., 401k) to their IRA. The Act also retained an individual's ability to convert a traditional IRA to a Roth IRA, thereby paying the income tax up front rather than at the time of withdrawal. Prior to doing so, these strategies should be reviewed with an individual's CPA in order to calculate the benefit which could be achieved over time, taking into consideration the amount of income tax that would be required to be paid at the time of the conversion.

10. How does the new tax law affect the transfer of business interests within a person's estate plan?

The Act had little change to the laws regarding the **transfer of business interests** through an estate plan. Some changes were made to the requirements of a trust making an election to be classified as a small business trust. The new rules now allow a non-resident alien to be a permissible shareholder if such an election is made. The Act did not change the requirement for an S corporation's shares to be held in a qualified subchapter S Trust that complies with the requirements for an S corporation under IRC Section 1361 (e.g., maximum number of shareholders and the requirement that income be passed through to the shareholders).

The transfer of the ownership of corporations and limited liability companies is an important aspect of proper estate planning. The proper titling of the shareholder's or member's interest must be integrated into an individual's plan. The determination of who will receive the business interest and who will manage a business after the owner's death or disability are important decisions. The use of customized buy-sell/restrictive stock agreements and customization of bylaws and operating agreements is vital to ensuring a business is continued or sold in an orderly manner.

11. How does the new tax law affect the use of insurance in an estate plan?

The Act had few changes **with regard to insurance planning within an estate plan** other than a few new requirements concerning the sale of insurance policies, for example, to an individual or from a trust. These rules would apply if the trustee of an irrevocable insurance trust wanted to sell a policy owned by the trust (such as to the beneficiaries or to another trust with different terms). These rules apply regardless of whether the policy is a term or whole life policy. The new rules will allow a portion of the sale to be reported as capital gains rather than as income. In the event of such a sale, the insurance company is now required to report the sale and basis to the IRS. Additionally, the parties to the sale are also required to report certain details of the transaction.

The transfer of insurance is still an important part of an estate plan as it can be utilized to pay for liabilities, fund business transfers, fund beneficiaries' trusts, equalize the inheritance between beneficiaries, and provide liquidity for the payment of income or estate taxes after death. The use of irrevocable insurance trusts, which will allow for the transfer of death benefits outside of an individual's taxable estate, are still encouraged if the size of the estate warrants their use.

12. May a conservation easement still be used for estate planning purposes?

Regarding **conservation easements**, which allows lands and properties to be held in designated trusts as conservation properties, recent case law has upheld the requirement for a transaction to be held under a perpetual easement. Any substitution of properties must be made only with comparable properties that qualify under the regulations. The estate and gift tax benefits available to the taxpayer by granting such an easement remain viable under the Internal Revenue Code and were unchanged by the Act.

13. May an irrevocable trust still be decanted?

A trustee of a discretionary trust may either modify an existing trust or establish a second trust by decanting a trust; recent case law has upheld a trustee's right to do so. If a trustee decides to decant assets from the original trust, i.e., the "first trust," by modifying the terms of the trust or constructing a new trust instrument, i.e., the "second trust," the trustee must adhere to the limits set forth under that particular state's decanting statute. In some jurisdictions other than Missouri, the courts have required the trustee to take into consideration the treatment of all the beneficiaries to ensure the trustee's actions were impartial and equitable to all the beneficiaries. In other jurisdictions, the courts have allowed the rule of impartiality be overwritten by the trust instrument and have allowed the beneficiaries of a trust to be changed. Decanting, by its nature, is a derivative of a trustee's power to make discretionary distributions based upon the trustee's determination alone; accordingly, a court should give a decanting trustee flexibility in exercising the power. When decanting, **best practices** would dictate that a trustee should carefully consider the reason for the change to the trust and the results to the affected beneficiaries.

14. May powers of appointments still be used in estate planning?

A **power granted to a beneficiary to appoint** the remainder of the beneficiary's trust assets during the beneficiary's life or at death is an important decision. In many instances the settlor will grant a beneficiary the right to appoint, i.e., direct, who will receive the balance of their trust at their death. The power to appoint may be general, allowing the beneficiary to appoint to any person, creditor of the beneficiary, the beneficiary's estate, or creditor of the beneficiary's estate. Likewise, the power to appoint may be non-general, limiting who the appointees may be (e.g., family members). In event the power is not exercised, the trust instrument should dictate who will receive the trust balance in default of the exercise. If such a power has been granted to a beneficiary, the flow of the trust fund must be analyzed. The power must be exercised by a written instrument, trust, or will in coordination with an individual's estate plan. A decision must be made determining who will end up with the property interest if the power is exercised or deferred. When exercising the power of appointment, attention must be given to any tax ramifications inherent in the exercise (for example, the extension of a generation skipping trust which was previously grand-fathered).

15. What changes have occurred in the Missouri trust or probate laws?

Missouri continues to modify its probate and trust laws to accommodate the changing needs of settlors, trustees, and beneficiaries. Recent amendments and proposed amendments to the **Missouri Uniform Trust Code** allow for fiduciaries to access digital assets, allow settlors to appoint trust protectors who may direct investments, allow beneficiaries to exercise powers of appointment, allow trustees to decant trust assets, and clarify numerous provisions that required technical corrections.

The proposed **Fiduciary Access to Digital Assets Act** allows personal representatives in probate estates, trustees administering trusts, attorneys-in-fact under powers of attorney, and conservators managing funds pursuant to a court appointment to access a person's or decedent's digital assets. Accordingly, pursuant to the proposed statutes, a fiduciary could be granted access to the digital information the person possessed or held before their incapacity or death. After the information has been accessed the fiduciary should be able to exercise their power to gain control of the underlying asset and administer it properly.

The proposed directed trust provision under the trust protector statute will allow a **trust protector** who has been granted the power under a trust instrument to **direct the trustee** how to invest or hold the trust assets. This power may be exercised in a manner which is different from what the trustee is normally required to do under fiduciary investment procedures. A trust protector's direction may allow a trustee to hold closely held business interests, invest in certain types of stocks or portfolios, or circumvent the normal diversification requirement that a trustee must follow. If a trust protector exercises these types of powers they will be held to a fiduciary standard, whereas the trustee will be exculpated from normal liability when following such directions.

The **Missouri Power of Appointment Act** specifies how a power to appoint trust assets may be accomplished by the beneficiary either during life or at the beneficiary's death. The differences between a general power and a non-general or limited power are clearly set forth. The manner in which a power may be designated in a trust instrument or will is clarified under the Act. Other topics, including creditor rights to property which made be appointed by a beneficiary and contingent beneficial rights that other parties may have, are delineated in the act as well. By understanding and following the act, Missouri practitioners should be given all the guidance necessary to properly draft and exercise powers to appoint and direct the distribution of property.

Powers of appointment can be used in many situations in order to grant a beneficiary the right to direct how the balance of a trust is to be distributed. The balance could be distributed to a limited number of beneficiaries (e.g. family members), or to any person, entity or taxing authority. This would allow, for example, a spouse to direct which children and what percentage interest each child would receive.

When establishing and exercising a power of appointment, the tax ramifications must be reviewed and analyzed, for example, whether the power of appointment will cause the trust assets to be included in the person's taxable estate. Powers of appointment can add flexibility to an estate plan and allow a beneficiary to change an estate plan after the settlor's death.

The proposed **Missouri decanting statute** has clarified numerous issues regarding a trustee's authority to exercise the power to change the terms of a trust or to transfer trust assets to another trust. This power may be exercised without a court order and allows a trustee to restructure a trust or establish a new trust for a permissible beneficiary.

16. What estate planning techniques are recommended as a result of the new tax law and Missouri trust law changes?

Based upon the changes made under the Tax Cuts and Jobs Act and Missouri Uniform Trust Code, several considerations should be made to ensure that a person's estate plan is current.

Because of the new estate, gift, and generation skipping tax law changes, only "wealthy" individuals will be required to consider the tax ramifications under their estate plan. Based upon each individual U.S. citizen being allowed to transfer $11,200,000 during their life or at their death (for calendar year 2018), most people can establish their estate plans without tax considerations being the driving force. Accordingly, the establishment of trusts to avoid probate, maintain assets, provide creditor protection, and to transfer assets in the precise manner desired by the settlor can be done with a focus on family and legacy planning.

For all married couples in Missouri, the use of a **qualified spousal trust** is still recommended based on the creditor protection granted from an individual spouse's creditor. This protection is derived from the tenancy by the entirety concept under Missouri law. A joint revocable living trust can be drafted to allow the surviving spouse to maintain complete control of the estate after the first spouse's death, or it can provide for separate shares between the spouses for particular planning objectives (e.g., distribution to differing family members or sheltering the decedent's share from the surviving spouse's creditors). Separate shares may also be established in order to allocate each spouse's generation skipping transfer tax exemption rather than relying on traditional joint ownership allocation rules.

Most parents express their concern for their children's ability to manage their inheritance and want to construct a distribution strategy that will protect the inheritance from creditors and predators (including lawsuits and divorce). Accordingly, Missouri law allows a settlor of a trust to draft the trust document to include a spendthrift clause, provide for discretionary distributions, and for perpetual legacies. A **spendthrift provision** may state that a beneficiary's' interest may not be subject to the claims of a beneficiary's creditors. Such a clause will prevent the assignment and attachment of trust assets from a lawsuit. In addition, a trust for a beneficiary may be established that allows the trustee to distribute income or principal within the trustee's sole and absolute **discretion.** Therefore, if a beneficiary is being sued or going through a divorce, the trustee may refrain from making a distribution after taking into consideration factors the trustee deems relevant. In making distributions, the trustee may also consider the beneficiary's resources and needs for health, education, maintenance, and support. As a result of the protection granted under discretionary trusts, it is recommended these techniques be reviewed in each situation. Finally, because a beneficiary did not establish such a trust for themselves, i.e., it is not "self settled," the beneficiary (including a spouse or child) may be the trustee of the trust established for their benefit and still retain the protections granted by a spendthrift provision and discretionary trust.

In consideration of the income and estate law changes, a review of the income tax ramifications and capital gains taxes must be made. Since the current law still provides for a **step-up in tax basis** for capital gains purposes at the death of an individual who owned those assets, planning must incorporate this analysis.

Under Missouri law, if spouses own property jointly, each spouse will receive a one-half (½) step-up in basis at each death, with the surviving spouse receiving a full step-up in basis if all the assets are included in the surviving spouse's estate. A full step-up in basis should occur if a simple joint revocable trust is used. Accordingly, in this scenario, if one spouse dies and property is sold it will receive a step-up in cost basis for one-half (½) of its value based upon the date of the deceased spouse's death. Therefore, it may be beneficial to plan for assets to be includable in the surviving spouse's taxable estate. This could be accomplished by simply transferring assets directly to the surviving spouse, but such a strategy could expose those assets to creditors and predators. In many cases, the better strategy would be transfer assets to a spouse in trust which would provide the surviving spouse with the beneficial enjoyment of the assets while simultaneously protecting those assets from future spouses and creditors. This could be accomplished through the use of a residuary trust or marital QTIP trust.

Under a **residuary trust** a surviving spouse could be given access for health, education, maintenance, and support, thereby excluding those assets from the surviving spouse's taxable estate. A residuary trust could also grant a surviving spouse a limited non-general power of appointment. The spouse could also serve as trustee and still receive the protection granted pursuant to a spendthrift trust. The trust could be discretionary or establish precise terms for distribution of income and principal. If, on the other hand, a spouse or beneficiary was granted a general power of appointment over a residuary trust, while the assets could be exposed to creditors or a claim in a divorce, the assets would be includible in the spouse's taxable estate and receive a full step-up in basis.

As an alternative, a spouse's distribution could be made to a **marital QTIP** trust which will automatically include the trust assets in the estate of the surviving spouse and grant a full step-up in basis at the death of the surviving spouse. A QTIP trust will require all of the income be distributed annually to the spouse and may allow for encroachments of principal to be made for the surviving spouse's health, education, maintenance, support, and comfort (since the assets are includible in the surviving spouse's estate). Under these circumstances a surviving spouse could be granted either a general or non-general (limited) power of appointment over the marital trust. If a power of appointment is granted, the surviving spouse could direct the distribution of the assets after his or her death.

A marital trust could also provide for a spouse to be granted the authority to disclaim all or part of the trust assets (within nine (9) months of the trust becoming irrevocable). A **disclaimer** of property interests will not allow a beneficiary to direct the subsequent distribution and therefore must allow the document to direct the distribution as set forth therein. Accordingly, a trust instrument may be drafted to provide that any part of a marital trust which is disclaimed will automatically fall to a residuary trust which may contain terms that differ from the marital trust. Such a strategy will increase flexibility for estate tax and capital gains planning. It should be noted that planning in reliance of disclaimer being made will require the surviving spouse or beneficiary to take action within the nine (9) month time limit.

The conversion of existing residuary trust assets (to assets that will be included in the surviving spouse's estate for capital gains purposes) may not be possible depending upon the terms and conditions of the existing residuary trust. It may be possible to convert existing trusts under the following circumstances (1) to swap out assets from a residuary trust if the power exists within the trust, (2) exercising a discretionary power previously granted, (3) to decant a discretionary trust, or (4) a trustee could seek a court reformation of the trust instrument.

Previously established trusts such a qualified personal residence trusts (QPRTs), grantor retained annuity trusts (GRATs), charitable remainder and charitable lead trusts (CLATs, CLUTs, and CLTs) will be hard or impossible **to unwind** without a court order. All of the options available to potentially achieve this type of conversion must be contemplated while taking into consideration both how the conversion will affect the beneficial interests that already exist as well as with regard to a trustee's fiduciary obligations.

It is impossible to know what is right for every person's estate plan without reviewing the exact facts and circumstances of that person's life, as every plan is different and should be customized to accommodate the wishes and desires of the individual. Each estate plan must also take into consideration the changes made under the Tax Cuts and Jobs act as well as the changes to the Missouri Trust Code. In addition, it is imperative for each individual to take responsibility to review the individual's estate plan on a regular basis to ascertain if the existing plan still meets the needs and wishes of the individual.

As a result of the new tax laws and trust law changes under Missouri law, an individual should immediately consider **reviewing their estate plan** in order to incorporate those changes into the individual's estate plan. In addition, as family circumstances change and personal assets evolve, periodic reviews of all existing plans and the funding of those plans must be made. Old documents may not have incorporated more recent laws or addressed circumstances that had not previously existed. Additionally, over time a person's goals and aspirations may have changed in response to evolving family dynamics.

Made in the USA
Monee, IL
04 November 2026

67383970R00134